Conflict Management in International Missions

This book serves primarily as a field guide and curriculum for organisations training personnel for conflict management missions abroad.

Currently, a gap exists between practitioners and academia in the field of conflict management and peacebuilding. Few practitioners have studied conflict management, and few academics have experience as field workers. Conflict literature contains a range of important insights and analyses, but is useful only to a limited degree to practitioners. This book provides practitioners with a much needed guidebook which is easy to understand, is academically solid and identifies with their mission and helps them relate to real-time challenges in the field. The book focuses on a number of case studies, including peacebuilding efforts in East Timor, and offers a range of practical advice for persons about to embark on a mission, from the receipt of an appointment to establishment in the field and encountering the realities and practical challenges that handling conflicts may imply.

This book will be of much interest to students of conflict management, peacebuilding and conflict resolution, as well as to practitioners in the field.

Olav Ofstad is an independent researcher and consultant in the field of conflict management, humanitarian assistance and development.

Security and Conflict Management

Series Editors:

Fen Osler Hampson

Carleton University, Canada

Chester Crocker

Georgetown University, Washington DC

Pamela Aall

United States Institute of Peace, Washington DC

This series will publish the best work in the field of security studies and conflict management. In particular, it will promote leading-edge work that straddles the divides between conflict management and security studies, between academics and practitioners, and between disciplines.

Negotiation and Conflict Management
I. William Zartman

Conflict Management and African Politics
Negotiation, mediation, and politics
Edited by Terrence Lyons and Gilbert M. Khadiagala

International Conflict Mediation
New approaches and findings
Edited by Jacob Bercovitch and Scott Sigmund Gartner

International Mediation in Civil Wars
Bargaining with bullets
Timothy D. Sisk

Conflict Transformation and Peacebuilding
Moving from violence to sustainable peace
Edited by Bruce Dayton and Louis Kriesberg

Theory and Practice of International Mediation
Selected essays
Jacob Bercovitch

UN Sanctions and Conflict
Responding to peace and security threats
Andrea Charron

Territorial Disputes and Conflict Management
The art of avoiding war
Rongxing Guo

Aid, Insurgencies and Conflict Transformation
When greed is good
Rob Kevlihan

Human Security in Turkey
Challenges for the 21st century
Edited by Alpaslan Özerdem and Füsun Özerdem

Understanding Complex Military Operations
A case study approach
Edited by Volker Franke, Karen Guttieri and Melanne A. Civic

Regional Organisations and Peacemaking
Challengers to the UN
Edited by Peter Wallensteen and Anders Bjurner

International Mediation Bias and Peacemaking
Taking sides in civil wars
Isak Svensson

Conflict Management in International Missions
A field guide
Olav Ofstad

Conflict Management in International Missions

A field guide

Olav Ofstad

Routledge
Taylor & Francis Group
LONDON AND NEW YORK

First published 2015
by Routledge
2 Park Square, Milton Park, Abingdon, Oxfordshire OX14 4RN

and by Routledge
711 Third Avenue, New York, NY 10017, USA

First issued in paperback 2017

Routledge is an imprint of the Taylor & Francis Group, an informa business

British Library Cataloguing-in-Publication Data
A catalogue record for this book is available from the British Library

Library of Congress Cataloging-in-Publication Data
Ofstad, Olav.
Conflict management in international missions : a field guide /
Olav Ofstad.
pages cm. – (Routledge studies in security and conflict management)
Includes bibliographical references and index.
1. Conflict management–Study and teaching. 2. Pacific settlement of international disputes–Study and teaching. 3. Peace-building–Study and teaching. I. Title.
JZ5534.O47 2014
303.6'9–dc23 2014029399

ISBN 13: 978-1-138-04810-2 (pbk)
ISBN 13: 978-1-138-79418-4 (hbk)

Typeset in Times New Roman
by Wearset Ltd, Boldon, Tyne and Wear

Contents

Acknowledgements

Those who find this book useful owe gratitude to a number of people. The foundations were laid in 2001 when I wrote the book 'Conflict management in international peace operations: a handbook for officers and soldiers' for the Norwegian Defence International Centre. A highly qualified project team was assigned to support me in the process. Colonel Hagrup Haukland contributed his comprehensive experience from various peace missions, and social anthropologist Anne Karin Nygård offered both scientific perspectives and insights based on humanitarian field missions. In addition to the team's support, I benefited from valuable comments from psychologist Henning Bang.

As I started developing the present book, Prof. Oliver Richmond, St Andrews, later Manchester University, offered invaluable comments on ethical perspectives and on the issue 'what kind of peace?'. Dr Leonard Goodstein, former CEO and Executive Vice President of the American Psychological Association, contributed important suggestions on mediation, and Prof. Robert Cialdini, renowned for his books on psychological influence, inspired me with generous comments on my application of social psychology.

Much of my peacebuilding research was connected to my fellowship at Oxford University in 2011, where my discussions with Prof. Jennifer Welsh and Prof. Richard Caplan allowed me to draw on their insights and analytical observations.

The East Timor peacebuilding process was an important part of my research, and Dr Benjamim Corte-Real, rector at the University of Timor Leste, and parliamentarian Manuel Tilman gave me essential briefings on East Timor's history. Dr Anthony Goldstone, General Michael Smith and Prof. Paulo Castro Seixas, all authors of books relevant to my work, readily commented on East Timor.

Isabel Guterres, Minister of Social Solidarity and former National Commissioner of East Timor's Commission for Reception, Truth and Reconciliation, together with Dr Joao Boavida, director of the Centre of Studies for Peace and Development (CEPAD), and Mariano Ximenes helped me acquire country-specific information on East Timor's conflicts and peacebuilding. So did Elisabeth Huybens, World Bank Country Manager in East Timor, and Laurianne Comard, Policy Officer on the Governance and Fragility Delegation of the European Union in Dili. Assistance was also rendered by Bishop Gunnar Stålsett,

Preface

Staff on international missions may experience conflict in a number of ways, ranging from the challenges of peace operations and third-party interventions to personal conflicts, falling out with local communities and exposure to attacks.

Handling conflict can be a complex and challenging task, and in hectic and challenging field missions we often have to make quick decisions.

Most of us are not skilled conflict managers. During my years in international missions I have been concerned by the lack of conflict management skills among international personnel. Evidently there is a need for support to make sound choices.

How can we access such support in critical situations? There is a wide range of literature addressing various aspects of conflict. Some of it is theoretical, offering comprehensive academic discussions with incisive analyses but limited practical conclusions. Some of it is more practical, offering advice on specific challenges found in peacebuilding, organisational or personal conflicts, communication and more.

It may, however, be a time-consuming and difficult task to find the advice needed, and field staff will often have to rely on their own judgement.

I came to think that it would be useful to provide struggling colleagues with a tool to manage conflict effectively; I envisioned a book tailored to the realities on the ground, transforming conflict theory into something tangible and practical. It should be a relatively brief, concise book, addressing typical field mission challenges, offering relevant advice when needed and a good overall understanding of conflict management.

In 2001 I wrote a book for the Norwegian Defence International Centre, which in 2003 was translated into English under the titles 'Conflict Management in International Peace Operations: A Handbook for Officers and Soldiers'. The feedback from military personnel was that this book offered advice needed in real-life situations, and met the needs of training curricula. The present book aims to do the same for all international personnel.

In addition to giving the reader a broad understanding of conflict management, I wish to make my own contributions to the field. In some contexts tools are offered that are not common in conflict literature. The chapter 'Influence: psychology versus traditional approaches' stands out in this context, transforming research results from social psychology into practical tools for peace.

Peacebuilding is an important part of the book, written with the hope of providing the reader with a good understanding of the topic. Discussing shortcomings and the need for improvement of today's practices, this chapter offers the reader concrete advice on a broad range of peacebuilding challenges, be it at a macro or a micro level.

While the book's target group is international personnel, anyone interested in expanding their perspectives and knowledge of conflict management should benefit from reading it. Much of the advice offered can in principle be used in any conflict context.

Olav Ofstad

Acknowledgements

Those who find this book useful owe gratitude to a number of people. The foundations were laid in 2001 when I wrote the book ‘Conflict management in international peace operations: a handbook for officers and soldiers’ for the Norwegian Defence International Centre. A highly qualified project team was assigned to support me in the process. Colonel Hagrup Haukland contributed his comprehensive experience from various peace missions, and social anthropologist Anne Karin Nygård offered both scientific perspectives and insights based on humanitarian field missions. In addition to the team’s support, I benefited from valuable comments from psychologist Henning Bang.

As I started developing the present book, Prof. Oliver Richmond, St Andrews, later Manchester University, offered invaluable comments on ethical perspectives and on the issue ‘what kind of peace?’. Dr Leonard Goodstein, former CEO and Executive Vice President of the American Psychological Association, contributed important suggestions on mediation, and Prof. Robert Cialdini, renowned for his books on psychological influence, inspired me with generous comments on my application of social psychology.

Much of my peacebuilding research was connected to my fellowship at Oxford University in 2011, where my discussions with Prof. Jennifer Welsh and Prof. Richard Caplan allowed me to draw on their insights and analytical observations.

The East Timor peacebuilding process was an important part of my research, and Dr Benjamim Corte-Real, rector at the University of Timor Leste, and parliamentarian Manuel Tilman gave me essential briefings on East Timor’s history. Dr Anthony Goldstone, General Michael Smith and Prof. Paulo Castro Seixas, all authors of books relevant to my work, readily commented on East Timor.

Isabel Guterres, Minister of Social Solidarity and former National Commissioner of East Timor’s Commission for Reception, Truth and Reconciliation, together with Dr Joao Boavida, director of the Centre of Studies for Peace and Development (CEPAD), and Mariano Ximenes helped me acquire country-specific information on East Timor’s conflicts and peacebuilding. So did Elisabeth Huybens, World Bank Country Manager in East Timor, and Laurianne Comard, Policy Officer on the Governance and Fragility Delegation of the European Union in Dili. Assistance was also rendered by Bishop Gunnar Stålsett, who found time in between his relentless peace work to appraise me of developments relevant to my book.

Among helpful UN representatives, I should mention the two former East Timor Special Representatives of the Secretary-General Ian Martin and Kamlesh Sharma, Deputy Special Representative of the Secretary-General Finn Reske Nielsen, Head of the UN Political Department in Dili Gary Gray, former head of the Department of PeaceKeeping Operations (DPKO) Dr J. M. Guehenno and Dr Endre Vigeland. I was also assisted by Vincent Kayijuka, Philip Helminger and Patrice Chiwota of the Peacebuilding Support Office, Stephen Jackson, Chief of Staff at the UN Office in Burundi and Dr Fred Babi, Senior Strategic Planning Officer of the UN integrated Peacebuilding Office in the Central African Republic.

The Burundi situation was further clarified by the assistance of Landry Ninteretse and Ruairi Nolan of Peace Direct, Burundi.

The book addresses a number of specific UN and World Bank practices unrelated to the above countries, and in this regard I was happy to draw on the knowledge of Jan Snoeks and Oliver Wittershagen of United Nations Volunteers, Bonn, as well as Koen Meyers, former representative of the UNESCO Jakarta office, and Patrick Barron, the World Bank Aceh.

As my work was nearing completion, Prof. Dominik Zaum, Reading University, generously shared his insights and offered a number of comments on the peacebuilding chapter.

Throughout my years of research and writing, I have benefited from discussions with psychologist Jan Sjøberg and researcher/consultant Paul Victor Wiker, both my colleagues in the context of conflict management training.

My wife Prabha has rendered consistent encouragement and contributed her experience from different peacebuilding missions, and Dr Evelin Lindner, the founder of the Human Dignity and Humiliation Studies, has been a never-failing source of inspiration. At the end of the process I found the comments from Routledge's anonymous reviewers very helpful.

Before submitting the final draft I drew on editing assistance from Shiraz Sidhva and Karan Chandran, supported by Nikhil Chandran.

To the extent that the book, despite all the high-quality support, contains flaws or lack of clarity, I am the only one to blame.

Olav Ofstad

Introduction

International missions relate to conflict in a variety of ways. Development work and humanitarian operations may take place in violent or post-violence settings, forcing agencies and staff to relate to conflicts. Peacekeeping missions are about addressing conflicts, and peacebuilding operations include a range of conflict management challenges. On an individual level, diplomats may be dispatched to address crises and, increasingly, international personnel are drawn into conflicts as parties, being exposed to threats and attacks. Even in generally peaceful environments, unforeseen conflicts may arise. Sometimes agencies or their staff fall out with the local community or authorities and have to terminate operations, and internal conflict between colleagues/superiors may frustrate progress and results.

All such challenges demand knowledge of constructive conflict management. The purpose of this book is to expand the reader's capability and understanding of peaceful conflict management and the possibilities of contributing to peaceful transformation.

The book provides a simple introduction to contemporary conflict theory and offers practical guidance on key approaches. Handling techniques and communication in conflict contexts are discussed with a view to the various kinds of conflicts international delegates may experience. In certain contexts, the book draws extensively on social psychology, transforming theoretical knowledge that is under-utilised in conflict literature into practical tools of influence.

The reader is introduced to the world of peacebuilding, and helped to acquire an overall understanding of concepts and practices. Peacebuilding is a subject under constant development, and this book suggests a need for further progress in a number of contexts. Among the examples picked from various peacebuilding efforts, the East Timor operations stand out as the only case where the UN was mandated to build a new state from scratch, and a number of experiences from East Timor are discussed.

The book offers a range of practical advice for persons about to embark on a mission, following him/her from the receipt of an appointment to establishment in the field and the encounter with the realities on the ground, including numerous principal and practical challenges that handling conflicts may imply.

While most of the advice is about third-party conflicts, that is, situations where we intervene in conflicts between others, guidance is also offered on handling one's own conflicts and security aspects related to them.

Target groups

This book is primarily meant for personnel working with international agencies or representing their government abroad. Some subjects will be more useful to leaders or senior personnel developing strategies, and others to employees working at grassroots level. Both civilian and military personnel engaged in peace missions will hopefully find the book useful. Some of the challenges of peacebuilding are similar to those peacekeepers face, but the perspectives of this book are broader.

In general, anyone assigned to an international mission in a conflict area should benefit from the information and advice offered. This includes humanitarian actors, consultants and even business employees. Moreover, many of the tools and techniques presented in this book will be appropriate in any conflict context, and the book would therefore be useful to anyone interested in the art of effective conflict management.

Contents

Chapter 1 presents the basic terms of conflict and conflict management. Chapter 2 is about preparing for a mission, whereas Chapter 3 offers advice on establishment in the field.

Next, Chapter 4 is a guide to mediation and facilitation, while Chapter 5 discusses the use of psychological influence for resolution of third-party conflicts versus traditional means of influence. Chapter 6 offers an introduction to the different aspects and challenges of peacebuilding and discusses practices that need development, whereas Chapter 7 presents the challenge of agencies and persons being party to a conflict, including security perspectives.

1 What you should know about conflicts

What is a conflict?

The definitions vary. A simple description is that a conflict arises when deviating positions or standpoints polarise two or more parties; in other words, when antagonism is caused by disagreement. Polarisation is to a large degree caused by the emotional elements of conflicts. One reason for this is that in conflicts we easily feel our interests are being threatened because they differ from those of our opponent.

Identification of interests is commonly considered key to conflict resolution, and many theorists limit the definition of conflict to the parties' perception or pursuit of incompatible aspirations.

However, at times we find antagonism, hatred and even violence among people without any visible difference of interest. Surprisingly, such relations are rarely included in the definition of conflict. For our purpose we shall include them. If we are to intervene constructively for peace, we need to address serious antagonism, interest-based or not. To this end we should try to understand what the antagonism is about, and in our terminology this means understanding the conflict. As we shall see later, we may at times handle conflicts without addressing the underlying reasons, but knowing them is always an advantage.

International conflicts are often categorised under such topics as: religion – ethnicity – ethics – politics – interests of power – race – gender – economy. These generally imply clashing interests related to these aspects.

How far such labels are correct may be established through conflict analysis. Popular perceptions are, however, often questionable. An example is the Bosnian war (1992–1995) which was frequently termed a religious/ethnic conflict, a view challenged in our discussion of ethnic and religious aspects. See p. 24.

A common notion is that conflicts at grassroots level, such as family contexts or organisations, are different from larger conflicts between ethnic groups or those on a high political level, and that something entirely different is required to handle these. Daily-life conflict experiences are not, in other words, relevant to international operations. This is a misunderstanding. We relate to human beings, their needs and emotions on every level. Even if some types of conflict are more complex than others as to issues, number of parties, etc., and demand more complex strategies, you may, to a large extent, use the same techniques regardless of the level at which you operate.

Interests, needs and antagonisms

Interests

Interests may be described as: concerns – expectations – motives – hopes – wishes – fears – needs.

'From position to interest' is a slogan in conflict management. The idea is that to resolve a conflict you have to know and address the various interests that caused it. This is very often true. It is important, however, to observe that depending on situation and technique one may also process conflicts constructively without addressing interests. The so-called brief therapy principles used by some therapists/consultants in family or organisational contexts basically disregard the reasons for the conflict and focus solely on solutions. (An introduction to the subject is offered by de Shazer, 1985.)

The reasons may also be irrelevant when exploring possible 'shortcuts to a solution' (p. 46, this volume) or applying tools of influence from social psychology as presented in Chapter 5. And we sometimes find that the interests that caused the conflict have been satisfied or forgotten, but prejudices or antagonism keep it alive.

Needs

Our most important interests are our basic human needs. Interests and needs may be defined as different terms, but for our purpose we consider our needs as part of our interests.

The definition of basic needs differs in different contexts, but factors often mentioned are: nourishment – accommodation – clothing – sex – identity – belonging – security – freedom – self-realisation – meaning of life – respect – understanding of others – recognition – positive self-image – understanding the outside world – activity – creativity – rest.

Conflicts often arise because we feel our basic needs are threatened, while on the surface the reasons for the conflict may appear to be different. Underneath each position one may find several layers of interests, with the basic needs at the bottom. For example, a party to a property conflict may have the chain of interests shown in Table 1.1

What on the surface appears to be a wish to own a property, here stems from the need for identity and respect. Sometimes we may find several different chains of needs underlying a position. We may, for instance, imagine that the person who wants to own a property is also motivated by its value and the need for financial security.

Although conflicts do not always derive from basic needs, the good conflict manager seeks to identify and keep the needs of the parties to the conflict in mind for three reasons:

Table 1.1 Chain of interests

Position:	To own property
Interests:	To build a cultural centre
	To arrange exhibitions and shows
	To make one's own culture known to others
	Identity and respect

- You need to find out to what extent the parties' needs are relevant.
- Peaceful solutions should not violate the parties' basic needs.
- Conflict management itself, including communication, has to take place in a way that considers basic human needs.

Some practical advice: when relating to parties in conflict, it may be useful if you, as part of your preparations, take a look at the list of basic human needs. Are human needs being threatened? How can you take these into consideration while handling the conflict?

Antagonisms

As indicated above, at times we find antagonism, hatred and violence among people who have no visible difference of interest. Factors that may spur animosity are:

- difference in values
- misunderstandings/misinformation
- lack of knowledge
- prejudices
- emotional vulnerability.

Sometimes underlying interests may have aroused the conflict but been later forgotten, and the antagonism has become a habit or part of a culture.

The remedy for antagonism is reconciliation and sometimes psychological influence, but we need to be aware that irrational antagonism is often mixed with conflicts of interests. Reconciliation efforts and conflict resolution may therefore have to go hand in hand.

Escalation, expansion and positive outcomes

A conflict is rarely a stagnant phenomenon, but changes with time, as to both content and intensity. As they tend to foster negative interaction, conflicts may easily escalate.

If we pursue our own interest at the expense of others, we will normally provoke a hostile reaction, which in turn provokes a hardening of our own intent. Consequently our feelings for the opponent turn increasingly negative, and harming the opponent may become as attractive as satisfying our own interests. In the worst case, our interaction turns violent.

Likewise, if we act on our prejudices, our own action and the action it provokes are likely to create negative spirals, worsening the conflict. (Psychological mechanisms related to negative acts are discussed in Chapter 5, see 'Cognitive dissonance').

The conflict may also become multidimensional, as we end up considering everything about our opponent to be bad or suspicious. This fact has implications for conflict interventions, as we may need to work simultaneously on a range of conflict aspects.

In early theory, conflicts were in general seen as problems to avoid. Later, the main question became how to resolve them. Today, it is common to focus on the positive potential. Constructive management of conflicts may release energy and resources and empower the parties as well as reveal new possibilities for development or cooperation.

The term 'conflict transformation' is therefore at times more appropriate than the traditional 'conflict resolution'. Pruitt and Rubin (1986: 6) offer three examples of such transition.

- Positive social change: reform processes often include conflicts that lead to constructive analysis, debates and progress.
- Reconciliation: sometimes the interaction following opposing claims leads to shared understanding and harmony.
- Group unity: if we recognise and confront issues of conflict among us, it may lead to a strengthened feeling of unity.

We might also add the possibility of personal gain and development, as conflicts sometimes bring the parties new and important insights.

These possibilities for a positive outcome represent an important aspect. As a conflict manager, you should relate to conflicts with an open mind. You do not necessarily have to resolve them. The challenge is to help those involved achieve the best possible outcome, no matter what this is. It could imply anything from calling off the disagreement to changes that render the conflict insignificant. It could be about sharing benefits or burdens, agreeing on cooperation or developing mutual understanding. Conflicts sometimes 'wither away' if the relationship between the parties improves. In brief, only your imagination sets the limits.

Conflict management terminology

The term 'conflict management' is used in different ways. Some consider it a negative term, about containing but not resolving conflicts.[1] Sometimes a wider definition is used, ranging from total submission to the use of physical force.

For our purpose, we shall use conflict management as a joint term for all conflict resolution and reconciliation activities, including any peace effort aimed at avoiding violence, reducing tensions or improving relationships.

Conflict resolution

The way we define it here, conflict resolution is any positive act or process aimed at ending the parties' pursuit of incompatible aspirations. By positive, we mean non-coercive, based on the parties' free will. In addition to such acts, we also use the term 'conflict resolution' for the end result, when the conflicting pursuits have ceased.

Some theorists apply a different definition, reserving the term 'conflict resolution' for efforts addressing the root causes of conflict with the aim of peaceful social and political change.

As this book also addresses personal conflicts, we shall not attach our definition to social and political change. Moreover, as shown later in the book, the pursuit of incompatible aspirations is sometimes brought to a peaceful end without addressing root causes, and such processes and results are included in our definition of conflict resolution.

Conflict transformation

As indicated above, conflict transformation differs from conflict resolution, being a process of transforming the parties' relationships, interaction and even interests towards elimination of antagonism, shared understanding and/or harmonious coexistence.

Reconciliation

After violent stages of conflict, victims are often left with feelings like hatred, bitterness and blame, sorrow, anger, shame, self-accusation and loss of trust in other people. Such burdens are a threat to sustainable peace. Reconciliation is a way of coming to terms with what has happened. Different from conflict resolution, this is a socialisation process that transforms negative feelings and changes adversaries' relationships from hostility and resentment to harmony and positive interaction. We may term it an interest-based kind of conflict transformation, although the interests are different from those that caused the conflict. The term may be used for the process, for the techniques we use to make it happen and for the end result. Essential elements are forgiveness and development of a feeling of 'we-ness' and loyalty.

Reconciliation may happen as a function of time, but we are going to focus on practical tools and techniques (see pp. 122–127).

If antagonism is connected to an interest-based conflict, both conflict resolution and reconciliation efforts may be needed.

Peacekeeping

This is a third-party intervention aimed at preventing violence and providing security. Such interventions may take place in acute crises or in situations where peace is under threat. In crisis situations peacekeeping operations are designed to ensure an environment where conflict resolution can take place and peacebuilding begin. Once a secure environment is established, peacekeeping is about ensuring the status quo.

Peacemaking

While the definitions of peacemaking vary, we shall reserve it for the process of bringing about a settlement between the parties to a conflict, be it through negotiation or through mediation. This implies a halt to violence, but is the beginning and not the end of the peace process, which normally depends on long-term peacebuilding.

Peacebuilding

The definitions of peacebuilding also vary. We are going to apply a broad definition in the sense that we include all non-violent, non-coercive efforts appropriate to move societies and human relationships towards peace, harmony and positive interaction. In principle, this also includes interventions at the peak of violence, and indeed, any conflict intervention should be conducted with a view to long-term peace. There is limited use in mediating a ceasefire if the parties start fighting again the moment you leave. While trying to contain war or violence we should, therefore, simultaneously look for ways to sustain and develop lasting peace. Some peacebuilding efforts can only take place in post-violence situations. Large-scale reconciliation is not possible in the middle of a war. The possibilities of long-term peacebuilding should, however, always be assessed as early as possible.

We use the term 'peacebuilding' both for single activities and for the sum of activities aiming at peace in a given context.

Some theorists include the objective of a just social order in the definition of peacebuilding, and as peacebuilders we should indeed try to contribute to just societies (see 'What kind of peace?', pp. 30–31). However, a just society implies justice, a need often abandoned at the expense of political stability. We may also submit that a just society implies democracy and fair distribution of wealth. The suggestion here is that we should be entitled to call our efforts peacebuilding even if a just social order is beyond reach.

To what extent is humanitarian assistance peacebuilding? If conducted in a peacebuilding situation, humanitarian activities might contribute to the peacebuilding process and be regarded as part of it, even if some humanitarian actors see this as an infringement of their neutrality. Regardless of this concern, it seems fair to expect humanitarian actors to be proponents of peace, and at a minimum observe the 'Do no harm' norms (pp. 148–151).

Statebuilding

This is a term for activities aimed at building a functioning state. It is primarily about building institutions, which normally means government and public administration, a legislative body, judiciary, police and security forces. The term also implies the training or education and recruitment of the staff required, and ensuring the control needed of the state's territory.

Statebuilding is not necessarily linked to peacebuilding, but as we shall see later, this may be an important component in UN peacebuilding operations. Like peacebuilding, the term may be used both for individual activities and for the cumulative process.

Development aid activities should not be confused with statebuilding. That is, statebuilding efforts such as infrastructure, school and hospital projects may be included, but development aid may also be about grassroots-level projects and changing mindsets for the purpose of empowerment and self-help.[2]

Nationbuilding

'When East Timor became independent, we should have come together and agreed on one objective, and one only, national unity' (former Timorese *liurai* (local king)) on the reasons for the peacebuilding collapse in 2006.[3]

Different from statebuilding, nationbuilding is about the development of a collective mindset, meaning a socialisation process where inhabitants of a given territory acquire a sense of national identity. This is an essential need in most peacebuilding equations, but one that is rarely adequately addressed.

Conflict and communication

How you communicate is essential to how you succeed in conflict management. Communication is therefore an overriding subject in this book. It is about both contents and form.

Our arguments or suggestions must be engaging or attractive enough to arouse interest, and the messages we forward must be sufficiently interesting for the recipient to want a dialogue. If, by contrast, the message is uninteresting, disgusting or frightening, it will normally not serve the purpose of peaceful conflict management.

This means that content must consider the needs and interests of the parties. You cannot suggest to a party that they lay down their arms if this would lead to a devastating attack on their village the next day. And an agreement is hardly sustainable if it implies a serious humiliation of one of the parties. The Versailles treaty is an example of this.

The importance of form is often neglected. Communication must have a form that complies with the needs of the parties, not least their needs for respect, understanding and appreciation, all of which are closely connected to our need to feel good about ourselves. Conflicts often escalate because these are ignored.

It may be difficult to meet such needs if, for example, your counterpart comes across as unreasonable or unpleasant, but it is normally possible to show respect and still express disagreement. Remember that we all need a positive self-image.[4]

Several of these elements will be discussed as we take a closer look at practical conflict management.

Is it possible to communicate respectfully and positively in any context? Depending on the purpose, we communicate differently in different situations. In a courtesy call and normal negotiations, politeness and respect may seem natural whereas in an acute crisis situation you might wish to make strong and direct demands. To take human needs into account when communicating is, however, a basic rule. Demands should therefore, as far as possible, be forwarded in a way that allows the recipient to feel respected.

Literature

While this book aims to convey essential knowledge on conflict management, its in-depth analyses are necessarily limited. For anyone interested in acquiring further and deeper knowledge, there is a rich variety of books on different conflict-related aspects. Among them, we might suggest the following selection.

General conflict understanding of conflict

- Pruitt, D. G. and Rubin, J. Z. (1986) *Social Conflict, Escalation and Settlement*, 3rd edition, New York: McGraw-Hill.

Mediation/negotiation

- Albrecht, K. and Albrecht, S. (1993) *Added Value Negotiating. The Breakthrough Method for Building Balanced Deals*, Homewood, IL: Business One Irwin.
- Fisher, R. and Ury, W. (1991) *Getting to Yes*, New York: Penguin Books.
- Moore, C. W. (2003) *The Mediation Process*, San Francisco: Jossey Bass.

Psychological influence

- Aronson, E., Wilson, T. D. and Akert, R. M. (1999) *Social Psychology*, New York: Addison-Wesley Longman.
- Cialdini, R. (1993) *Influence. Science and Practice*, New York: Harper Collins.
- Rosenberg, M. B. (1999) *Nonviolent Communication. A Language of Compassion*, Del Mar, CA: Puddle Dancer Press.

Peacebuilding

- Anderson, M. (1999) *Do No Harm: How Aid Can Support Peace – or War*, London: Lynne Rienner.
- Deutsch, M. and Coleman, P. T. (2000) *The Handbook of Conflict Resolution. Theory and Practice*, San Francisco: Jossey Bass.
- Lederach, J. P. (1997) *Building Peace: Sustainable Reconciliation in Divided Societies*, Washington, DC: United States Institute of Peace.
- Reychler, L. and Paffenholz, T. (2001) *Peacebuilding, A Field Guide*, London: Lynne Rienner.

Notes

1 Galtung (1985) introduced the term 'negative peace' for such situations.
2 For a deeper understanding of the many aspects of statebuilding, see Caplan (2012).
3 Interviewed by the author in June 2011.
4 Lindner (2006) made a compelling presentation on humiliation as a cause of conflict in international settings.

References

Caplan, R. (2012) *Exit Strategies and State Building*, New York: Oxford University Press.

de Shazer, S. (1988) *Clues. Investigating Solutions in Brief Therapy*, New York: W. W. Norton.

Galtung, J. (1985) 'Twenty-five years of peace research: ten challenges and some responses', *Journal of Peace Research* 22(2).

Lindner, E. (2006) *Making Enemies Unwittingly: Humiliation and International Conflict*, London: Praeger Security International.

Pruitt, D. G. and Rubin, J. Z. (1986) *Social Conflict, Escalation, Stalemate and Settlement*, New York: Random House.

2 Preparing for missions

Let us start with the situation where you have received an assignment. The following advice is given with a view to preparing you for conflict management tasks, but most of it will be of relevance for preparations for missions abroad in general.

Hopefully you will be enthusiastic about the chance of supporting a country or a people in need, but there are parameters and conditions you need to observe. One thing is your own qualifications for the job. Another is allegiances and principal obligations, some defined in your job description, others in international instruments and some unwritten. These set terms for your work and will be discussed in this chapter.

So will power equations and legitimacy, local culture, traditions, religion and ethnicity, all factors that may influence your work. While international personnel are sometimes able to make important differences, we need to combine our enthusiasm with realism.

Personal qualifications

Professional demands

Are you qualified for the job? You should ask yourself this question before accepting an assignment with an international mission. (Although this may sound obvious, you are likely to meet delegates who have never asked themselves this). If the answer is no, you should immediately inform your employers to be. Unless you can switch to a job you are qualified for, you should withdraw.

In times of emergency, organisations sometimes recruit personnel uncritically. After the 2004 tsunami, many young first-timers were sent to Aceh, known for its protracted violent conflict. Some were sent to islands off Sumatra such as Nias and Simulue. Both islands have a humid climate, known to be demanding to westerners, and much of the work would take place in the jungle. Nias was known to have a demanding cultural climate, and some humanitarian actors withdrew from the island after a while because of threats from locals who were not included in support programmes.

What will your working environment be like? Are you resilient and mature enough to be comfortable and effective in a precarious environment? Can you take the stress of a conflict zone where you are viewed with suspicion or have problems relating to the local culture? Will you have supportive colleagues around you? What are the routines for rest and recreation (RnR) and access to medical facilities?

Realism suggests that you assess your own qualities in the light of the working environment that awaits you before signing the contract.

What language will be used in the mission? A good command of the actual working language both verbally and in writing is mandatory. Be critical of yourself when assessing this issue. If you lack the skills required, the mission could become a nightmare for you and a liability for your employer.

Personal motives

Let us assume that your desire to help people in need is the main reason you accepted your assignment, and that you are committed to your mission. There may, however, be factors that distract you from this commitment.

One possible threat is cynicism. If you find yourself working with problems you cannot solve, and see no way you can contribute to making a meaningful difference, it is very easy to become cynical, thinking, 'OK, it does not really matter what I do in this job. I might as well hang around as long as I am comfortable.'

Even if you succeed in your work, precarious environments may burn you out and wear down your spirit.

Another risk is de-motivation spurred by disagreement with your agency's directions or overall peacebuilding policies (see 'Allegiances and responsibilities' below). If, for instance, you disagree with the objective of replacing a council of elders with party-based rule, or with a plan to move from subsistence farming to export-oriented agriculture, your commitment may suffer.

Sadly, it appears that personal economy and personal perks can be another distracting factor. You may meet well-paid delegates who happily discuss salary levels and what they mean to do with their savings, but show precious little commitment to contributing to peace and development.

To ensure the spirit you need throughout your mission, and to give the agency employing you value for its money, it is essential to think through your commitment and attitude early on.

- Why am I accepting this job?
- What are my personal drivers?

You should examine your personal motivation at intervals. Ask yourself if anything has changed. Are you still there for the right reasons, as committed as you need to be? It may also be useful to discuss this topic with colleagues.

Allegiances and responsibilities

Since we assume that you have accepted your assignment out of concern for the people of the country or region in question, a basic allegiance is a given. This allegiance should inform all your professional activities. In addition, there will be your allegiance to your employer, and there might be another to the entity funding your activities. As if this were not enough, you might feel an allegiance to the UN or other major peace operators, and, perhaps more or less unconsciously, to the values of the culture you come from. There is no guarantee that these allegiances point in the same direction.

Imagine that you have taken up your post and are convinced that there is a need for a large-scale youth programme, involving combatants and unemployed youth in dialogue and cooperation for peace. Your agency has the money and you know you can do it. Your organisation believes, however, that you should focus on education, and your funding agency believes a military academy would be desirable, something you do not think is going to serve peace.

Different views on priorities are common. You might opt to 'fight' for your view, but the military academy is perhaps the most likely outcome. This means that you will have to make the best of it if you want to stay in the job. Subject to your luck or seniority, you may be involved in strategic assessments and allowed to exert influence on choice of direction, but most international personnel should expect such challenges.

In addition to allegiances there are a number of parameters that will influence your work. And some of them might define quite concretely what you are supposed to do.

Job description and plans of action

A job description defining your mission should be in place for most missions that have been established in an area for some time. In emergency missions, this is not always so. In this case, ask for one. Study the job description carefully and discuss anything unclear with your employer.

Sometimes your arrival may overlap with your predecessor's mission. If so, use the time optimally to get the best possible update. You should get a handover memo from your predecessor. If you do not, ask for one. Be specific on what you desire. Conflicts relevant to your assignment should be part of the memo, as should details of the relationship with civilian authorities and cooperating partners.

Is your organisation involved in peacebuilding? If so, an outline of the current situation, achievements and challenges is required. If your work is going to include particular cases or problems, request that the memo contain a short summary on each case. A reference to informative analyses and reports is also useful.

There may be overriding goals and frames for the actual mission, laid down in plans of action or other documents describing the operation. If not, you should raise this with your employer. If you have to contribute to such plans yourself once you are out in the field, it will cost you time and effort, but the advantage is that you can influence your scope of work.

Documents defining peace operations

Both peacekeeping and peacebuilding operations are supported by documents that legitimise the international intervention. These will contain important information for all actors participating in the operations. The following documents are significant.

Resolution by the UN Security Council

This gives the mandate for international intervention. The mandate may be given to UN missions, but also other major peace operation actors. In Bangui, capital of the Central African Republic, hit by a violent internal conflict in March 2013, a UN peacebuilding mission was assisted by an African Union peacekeeping operation, supported by a French force, and in January 2014 an EU force was mandated to join the operation.

UN mandates are sometimes not very clear and may miss elements that are important to peacebuilding processes (see p. 104). Reconciliation has, for example not been consistently included, even when the UN does conduct reconciliation efforts.

Such documents may, however, contain important terms that international organisations need to know about.

Agreement between the UN and the host country

While defining frames of cooperation between the host country and the UN, such a framework should be observed by all international actors.

Analyses and peacebuilding plans

To the extent that analyses of peacebuilding needs or conflict analyses are available, you should read them in conjunction with possible peacebuilding plans. However, as you will find later in this book, such analyses may be missing.

If the government in charge has a proper peacebuilding plan, this is essential reading, but unfortunately such plans are rare. If the UN Peacebuilding Commission is involved, you may find a Priority Plan for Peace and a Framework for Peacebuilding, perhaps also supporting matrices with objectives, activities and indicators. The Framework for Peacebuilding is meant to be an expression of shared priorities between the government and the UN. You should definitely read these documents, even if this book suggests that an evaluation of UN planning practices is called for.

Development plans

While adequate peacebuilding plans are often missing, government development plans and poverty reduction strategies may contain valuable information. Such plans may also include some peacebuilding elements, although often in quite general terms.

UN reports

Reports on UN peacebuilding efforts in the country or region are an essential source of information and contribute to the definition of missions, justifying changes or renewed efforts. Normally available on the web, they also give you an overall picture of what the UN and the government are doing, offering important updates on challenges and progress.

International instruments and norms

Whether mentioned in your job description or not, certain international instruments should inform your work at all times. Some of these are international law. Other documents, such as strategies or guidelines developed by different actors on the international arena, could also contain norms your agency is committed to respect. In general, if an agency funds your organisation's activity, you must follow its norms.

Human rights

The Universal Declaration of 1948 defines a number of rights that we are all obliged to respect. Even so, some of them, such as the right to education, work and social security, are still distant goals in poorer parts of the world.

Other important rights are more a matter of attitude and often deliberately violated. Examples are the right to life, protection against arbitrary arrest, the right to a full and fair public hearing by an independent and impartial tribunal, the individual's right to decide about entering marriage, the right to freedom of thought and expression, the right to freedom of religion and the right to participation in government, directly or through representation.

One of the Declaration's fundamental norms, expressed in Article 1, states that all human beings are born free and have equal rights. In this perspective, we should be aware of the United Nations Security Council Resolution 1325 of 2000,[1] which underscores 'the important role of women in the prevention and resolution of conflicts and in peace-building', and stresses the importance of 'their equal participation and full involvement in all efforts for the maintenance and promotion of peace and security'. The Resolution also calls on all parties to armed conflict to take special measures to protect women and girls from gender-based violence.

Another set of norms complementing the Human Rights Declaration is the United Nations Convention on the Rights of the Child of 1989 and two Optional Protocols of 25 May 2000 – essential parameters in peace and development equations. For an easy introduction to this issue, see Narayan (undated).

How do these norms affect us in practice? Some actors have taken a human rights approach to peacebuilding (p. 96), while, unfortunately, others appear to avoid relating to human rights. Clearly, our own activities and those of our partners must not violate or neglect human rights. To this end both proactive measures and responses to violations might be required.

Whether we develop a programme or agree to support another actor, we should make sure that respect for human rights is reflected in the plans. Proactive measures could also imply advocacy, monitoring/reporting, and initiatives for institutional reform that strengthens human rights.

On the response side we might typically need to react to gross discrimination, crimes against children and sexual and gender-based violence.

As we shall see below, standing up for human rights can be a challenge, at both micro and macro levels.

International Humanitarian law and the Responsibility to Protect

Humanitarian law regulates conduct in armed conflicts in terms of protecting civilians and restricting/regulating the means of warfare and treatment of prisoners of war. These norms of international law are found in the Geneva conventions and the Hague conventions, subsequent treaties, case law and customary law.

The Responsibility to Protect is a set of norms endorsed by the UN Assembly member states at the World Summit of 2005 and later clarified by the secretary general in a number of reports.[2]

The norms include:

- the responsibility of states to protect their population from genocide, war crimes, crimes against humanity and ethnic cleansing;
- the responsibility of the international community to support states in fulfilling this responsibility, but also to intervene through diplomatic, humanitarian and other means to protect populations from such crimes.

The RtoP norms on external intervention are not yet commonly accepted as international law, and the international community's right to military intervention is a subject of debate.

For our purpose we need to know that the norms suggest a moral responsibility not only for state actors. International agencies should observe the RtoP in programme/implementation contexts, but should also take action to protect exposed populations when necessary.

Acting on this responsibility, a number of NGOs and institutions world-wide have joined forces in the International Coalition for the Responsibility to Protect. This coalition's commitment includes mobilization of NGOs 'to push for action to save lives in RtoP country-specific situations'.[3]

We shall not discuss our RtoP obligations in detail. However, natural duties for most of us in case of violations would be to monitor and report to our line of command, while in case of emergency we may also have to take an immediate diplomatic initiative, with central or local government, or even with military forces or armed groups. See an example on p. 88.

OECD/DAC norms

The Organisation for Economic Cooperation and Development (OECD), a group of 34 countries dedicated to global development, has developed several guiding documents on international support to development and peacebuilding. Among the essential ones are:

- *The Security Sector Reform Handbook* (OECD, 2007), a comprehensive, widely acknowledged guide to transformation/development of the justice sector, presenting concrete approaches as well as principles;
- the OECD Convention on Combating Bribery of Foreign Public Officials in International Business Transactions (1997),[4] which is binding on its signatories;
- the OECD's Development Assistance Committee (OECD, DAC, 1999), *Guidelines for Gender Equality and Women's Empowerment in Development Cooperation*, which offers comprehensive advice on gender integration, including gender equality strategies for DAC members;
- OECD, DAC (2011) *Supporting Statebuilding in Situations of Conflict and Fragility: Policy Guidance*, a document that discusses a range of state- and peacebuilding concepts and offers advice on policies, but also on concrete tasks such as designing a country programme.

The World Development Report 2011 on Conflict, Security and Development

This comprehensive World Bank report offers analysis of conflict perspectives in the twenty-first century in a global perspective. Highlighting the needs of fragile states, the report suggests directions for international support globally, regionally and locally. In a roadmap for breaking cycles of violence at country level, the report presents policy and programme tools for country actors. Job creation, security and justice are emphasised as essential tools to break cycles of violence.

G7+ and The New Deal

The High Level Forum on Aid Effectiveness, gathered in Busan in 2011, was also the venue for the G7+, an association of 17 conflict-affected states established in 2010.[5] Together with international partners, the G7+ issued *The New Deal*, a document suggesting five standardised goals for peace- and statebuilding. This approach, which by January 2013 was endorsed by 35 countries and six international organisations including the UN Development Group and the World Bank,[6] is discussed in Chapter 6.

EU norms

The EU's voluntary *Code of Conduct on Complementarity and the Division of Labour in Development Policy* (2007) aims at improved coherence and structure in development aid, offering 11 general principles of cooperation. These may also influence development aid in a peacebuilding context, see 'Choice of activities' in Chapter 6 (p. 101).

The *Concept on Strengthening EU Mediation and Dialogue Capacities* (2009), which lays down parameters for mediation efforts, should also be noted.

An EU-funded publication of value to delegates is the handbook *In Control* (Lauffer *et al.*, 2013).

OSCE, Human Dimension Commitments

If you happen to work for the 57-member Organisation for Security and Cooperation in Europe, which is a major humanitarian actor, the OSCE's *Human Dimension Commitments* (2005) is one of the publications you should know about. This document discusses protection of human values and human rights, linking them to institutional aspects. The OSCE's expressed view is that 'pluralistic democracy based on the rule of law is the only system of government suitable to guarantee human rights effectively'.[7]

Red Cross/Red Crescent principles

While the above organisations generally have humanitarian values more or less implicit in their statutes or strategies, the Red Cross/Red Crescent Movement has adopted seven fundamental principles that all staff are obliged to adhere to.[8] We shall not discuss these in detail here, but two principles related to conflict management need attention.

IMPARTIALITY

In a Red Cross/Red Crescent context, impartiality means non-discrimination on the basis of nationality, race, gender, religious beliefs, class or political opinions. This is clearly a principle that all international workers should adhere to.

NEUTRALITY

Does third-party conflict management require that you are neutral, meaning that you do not take sides in conflicts? Not necessarily, unless your organisation is committed to this principle. The UN refugee agency UNHCR's mandate to pursue protection, assistance and solutions for refugees may necessitate a clear stand against a party trying to expel refugees from an area. Still, the UNHCR may be accepted as a mediator between the two groups. The crucial issue will normally be whether you are respected for the principles you stand for and are trusted to conduct your role with fairness and integrity.

Legitimacy and power

Governments we support should be legitimate. Legitimacy is commonly considered a requirement for peace and long-term stability, and a safeguard against violence.

'Risks of violence are greater when high stresses combine with weak capacity or lack of legitimacy in key national institutions, as shown by the recent turbulence in the Middle East and North Africa', according to a World Bank press release on the 2011 *World Development Report*.[9]

The problem, however, is that legitimacy is not a clear-cut term. Papagianni (quoted in DFID, undated: 16) defines states as legitimate when elites and the public accept the rules regulating the exercise of power and the distribution of wealth as proper and binding.

If we apply this definition, we must observe that there are degrees of acceptance. Both tolerating and welcoming the rules may fall within the frames of acceptance, and the percentage of people accepting them generally changes with time.

Acceptance will normally depend on factors like performance and results, meaning economic growth, public services, human rights and distribution of wealth, type of governance (democracy vs dictatorship) and people's attitude to these factors.

Democratic elections may ensure legitimacy, but they do not necessarily do so. This was well demonstrated in Egypt, Thailand and Ukraine in 2013/2014, where large numbers of people rejected democratically elected governments, accusing them of abusing their positions. Development aid and peacebuilding work may witness slow changes in a government's legitimacy or rapid ones as in the case of coups. How should we relate to decline or loss of legitimacy?

If your activities imply limited or no support to the government, the answer might be easy. For instance, if you run a food programme in a drought-stricken area ignored by the government, its legitimacy will normally be of little consequence.

To the extent that we do support the government, the situation becomes more complex. We may pull out, change our activities or continue as before. On a macro level the assessment can be quite difficult and the option of pulling out problematic. In fragile countries termination of a peacebuilding process might lead to disaster.

On a micro level we also need to take the overall peace and development perspective into account, but the scope of concrete consequences may be limited.

- If you are supporting the training of security forces in a promising democracy exposed to a coup, and discover that the new rulers will use the forces to establish as dictatorship, you may find it easy to pull out.
- If your agency is upgrading the courts in a country where democracy is deteriorating, and the judiciary is increasingly serving the interests of the president's party, you may wish to put your agency's money elsewhere. You

might, however, have to make a difficult assessment, weighing the gains against negative consequences, on both macro and micro levels.

The point here is to beware of the legitimacy aspect. As in many other peace and development contexts, being conscious and conscientious is the best we can do.

'Do no harm'

Your mission may include the distribution of aid, and if this happens in a conflict zone, the distribution is likely to have effects on peace. The conflicts may also influence your work directly. The 'do no harm' concepts, presented in Mary Anderson's book (1999), are about these aspects. The book offers important advice on how to avoid negative effects and achieve positive ones. For aid workers it is a must to know about the 'do no harm' concepts; in fact anyone involved in peace-related work should know about them. (See the discussion of 'do no harm' on pp. 148–151.)

The need for local knowledge

Peacebuilding, conflict resolution, humanitarian emergency missions and development aid are all about influencing reality, and a good grip on the reality we want to influence is essential. Our grip should include basic knowledge of the relevant country's history, culture, traditions and religion. Unfortunately, this requirement is commonly neglected. Delegates are sent to conflict areas without much prior knowledge, and given little opportunity to acquire it before the challenges of work demand all their attention.

Lack of knowledge and understanding of local situations can in the worst case be disastrous. The collapse of the East Timor peacebuilding process in 2006 is possibly one such example (see Ofstad, 2012). While it is the responsibility of the peacebuilding leadership to ensure the knowledge needed for the principal decision-making, the viewpoint here is that anyone trying to contribute to peace and development should make an effort to acquire the knowledge needed for their work.

History

This often ignored element may hold information crucial to peaceful change and development, and the history of conflicts must always be observed.

When the peace- and statebuilding process started in East Timor in 2002, the international community appeared to give little attention to the island's 400-year history of violent internal conflict. These conflicts were partly about ethnic/geographical rifts but were also connected to the different groups' relationships with colonial powers/occupiers. These factors contributed to the havoc in 2006, described in Chapter 6, which ended what had been widely considered a UN peacebuilding success story.

History may also shed light on the positions and attitudes of parties and stakeholders. The parties' perceptions may differ dramatically. Serbs and Kosovo-Albanians generally appear to have very different perceptions of Kosovo's demographic history, as Kosovo-Albanians seem to consider their own existence in Kosovo older and more established than the Serbs do (Jansen, 1999). Making up your own mind on such topics may require more time than you have. But for your work it may be enough to have a clear understanding of the views of the parties and stakeholders.

History may indicate both future possibilities and obstacles to peace. If you wish to render support to political development or the establishment of conflict resolution mechanisms, you should know what institutions existed in the past. Was there perhaps a system of councils of elders governing society or handling conflicts? If so, how did this system function? Did it meet people's needs? Does it make sense to build on such past practices, or do people need something different today?

In a reconciliation perspective, we discuss the importance of 'connectors and dividers', elements that bring people together or split them (Chapter 6, p. 145).

If something worked between the parties before, we might draw on it for reconciliation purposes, while factors that caused divisions should in general be avoided.

Culture

An engineer working for NORAD on a hydropower feasibility study in Tangir, northern Pakistan, in the early 1990s came out of his hut one morning and decided to take some photos of the beautiful landscape. Shortly after, a man turned up with an AK 47 and wanted to kill him. It turned out that this man's wife had been out in the landscape the engineer was photographing, and his colleagues had to enact some frenetic diplomacy to save his life.

Culture may be defined as the ideas, customs, and social behaviour of a particular people or society.[10] While violations of cultural norms rarely kill us, observing them is generally important to our professional success and wellbeing.

Some manifestations of culture, such as art, literature, music, sports, dress codes and cuisine, are easily observable and are often called the tip of the iceberg. Most of the factors that matter to you as a delegate are found beneath the surface. Many of them are essential for your ability to interact without friction and be accepted in local society. Examples are: roles related to gender, age, class, profession; codes of modesty and politeness; concepts of sin; notions of duties, rights and privileges; norms of social appropriateness in interaction, including use of titles, body language, handshakes, eye contact, physical space, loudness; frequency of social interaction; observance of holidays; religious and spiritual customs; and much more.[11]

While these factors may decide success or failure both socially and in work situations, there are other more 'work-specific' aspects, such as concepts of leadership, authority and hierarchy; cooperation vs competition; assertiveness vs listening; levels of directness; concepts of 'keeping the floor'; perceptions of logic and validity; notions of time and speed of work.

Some UN agencies such as UNESCO, the DPKO and United Nations Volunteers (UNV), as well as some UN military missions, may provide cultural training for their personnel, but outside the UN family such training is rare. For general insights there is a rich literature available. (Useful examples are Oberg, 1960 and Storti, 1994.) But to gain a proper understanding of the culture you are going to work in, you may have to explore local possibilities of training. (See 'Lectures/seminars?', p. 29.)

While the scope of this book does not allow for a discussion of the numerous cultural challenges we may face, it is worth observing some aspects that could become a problem in programme contexts.

Democracy

You may consider party-based democracy an obvious model of governance, and it may be your professional duty to promote it. Your local counterparts might, however, have different ideas. Their country or region may have a history of poverty, violence and insecurity, where allegiance to a mighty warlord was the best chance of survival. They may also have found security and support in their tribe, clan or family. To them, it may seem very unlikely that politicians and parties outside such spheres of loyalty will care for their interests.

Particularly if the country is deeply divided, people may find democracy a risky experiment, a view we can hardly term irrational. As discussed in Chapter 6, democracy in war-torn countries often becomes a war by other means. As outsiders, we can only render meaningful support to political development if we understand such perspectives[12] (see also 'What kind of peace?' pp. 30–31).

Gender

It will normally be our professional obligation to support gender equality, but if our counterparts have a long tradition of gender imbalance, such ideas may sound outlandish. Meaningful initiatives on this matter require tact and caution. If we start out with strong statements, for instance on the ethics of the subject, we might easily come across as arrogant and condescending, something that inevitably jeopardises cooperation.

Youth

Addressing the situation of youth is generally important in peacebuilding contexts. This is about getting them off the streets and into gainful activities. Job creation is often a key, but you might also have ideas of engaging youth in political dialogue and in processes that give them a sense of being part of the country's development. You could, however, be in for a challenge. While youth are commonly exploited as fighters, many societies have little regard for them as participants in public debate and the development of society.

Child labour

This is a common phenomenon in many poor countries, and while we find it disturbing, our local interlocutors may depend on it for the family's survival. So while we may wish to advocate for the welfare of the child and the importance of education, our arguments may be rejected as hollow unless we can suggest and perhaps contribute to alternative ways of sustaining the family.

Religion and ethnicity

These aspects of culture are considered common causes of conflicts. To some extent this view is justified. Some conflicts, such as the Shia–Sunni conflict, are rooted in religion. Ethnicity plays a role in many conflicts, such as in the Israel–Palestine conflict or the antagonism against Roma people found in many European countries. To the extent that ethnicity is associated with race, such conflicts are easily infected by aspects of racism.

However, as earlier indicated, conflicts are sometimes termed religious or ethnic, even if there is nothing in the parties' ethnic background or religion that causes disagreement. The Bosnian war (1992–1995) was fought over territory and life. The reason why it took place was probably that the parties felt their essential needs, like economic and social security, justice, identity and more, were being threatened.

When conflicts escalate, we are inclined to look around for support. It becomes natural to seek others in the same situation. Identity then becomes not only a need in itself, but also a means to strengthen one's own group. To reinforce identity we may focus on factors like ethnic background and religion. The conflict may then appear to others as ethnic/religious, even if there is nothing in the parties' ethnic or religious background that constitutes a threat or problem to others. The tendency to look for simple explanations like religion, ethnicity and race often causes the real, underlying reasons to be disregarded. As indicated above, these reasons very often pertain to interests and needs.

The parties' perception of the conflict is also influenced by what they do. If both sides seek refuge/support in religious or ethnic groups, they may come to perceive the conflict as religious or ethnic, even if it initially evolved over non-religious issues such as resources and security.[13]

As observed in the discussion of history above, the parties' perceptions are essential. And images of 'us versus them' may link mistrust and hatred to ethnicity.

Religious actors sometimes play an important role even if the conflict has little to do with religion. Buddhist monks were an important stakeholder in Sri Lanka's war between the government and the Tamil Tigers. The East Timor

Catholic Church was an important resistance force during the struggle with Indonesia, even if the essence of the conflict was national independence. When we try to build peace we should always consider the need to involve major religious actors.[14]

Seeking information

You may have little time for preparations. Still, you may have more time to access information at home than out on the mission. Use the time you have before your departure to get information about the mission and the challenges ahead.

The briefing materials provided by your employer may be a starting point, but you normally need more. Use the web actively. Seek articles on the above subjects. If possible, contact your superior to be and your predecessor to get a picture of what awaits you and what you should prepare for in particular. What can they tell you about the area and its conflicts? What interaction has been established between the international organisations and other actors?

You may also contact other resource persons who are in the field or have been there, either for other civilian organisations, your country's embassy or peacekeeping forces. Such contacts may be particularly important if your organisation is new to the area.

Possibilities for cooperation

Has cooperation been established between local authorities and international organisations? If not, what is the scene and what are the possibilities? What organisations in the area could be considered for cooperation? Are there peacekeeping forces in the field? What local actors could be your partners? Ask for your employer's view on existing interaction and possibilities. You might also discuss the cooperation issue with civilian organisations or military representatives from your own country if they are part of the peacekeeping forces.

Principles under pressure

Let us assume you have prepared well for your mission. You have discussed your job description, plans and essential aspects with your employer. You have linked up with your predecessor, assessed cooperation possibilities in the field and studied key documents. You have also made an effort to acquaint yourself with historical and cultural aspects, and studied the norms and principles that you need to observe in your work.

So what can go wrong? We have earlier observed that you should match your enthusiasm with realism. One reason is that field work often implies dilemmas and pitfalls. A variety of unforeseen developments may threaten both your results/achievements and the values and principles you intend to pursue. Let us look at some examples:

- Your organisation is funding an education programme for boys and girls in equal numbers, and you discover after the beginning of the school year that nearly all the enrolled students are boys. What do you do? Demand that the programme be stopped or make the best of it?
- You find that some 20 per cent of your agency's funding of a business credit programme is being siphoned off. Otherwise the programme is working well, and a number of small businesses have emerged. There is reason to suspect that the prime minister's wife is involved in the scam. What do you do?
- You learn that about half of the emergency provisions provided by your agency have been stolen by a group of brutal insurgents, strengthening their ability to fight. The other half is benefiting a group of civilians who may starve to death without the support. It seems impossible to stop the thefts. What do you do?
- You are working in a country where insurgency erupts. The government is democratically elected but oppressive, abusing human rights, and the insurgents appear to be fighting for genuine democracy. Your food programme is operating in an area controlled by the insurgents and, by continuing it, you are indirectly supporting them. Do you continue the programme?

There is in principle no limit to possible situations where you face problems relating to your job description, allegiances and essential norms and values.[15] And there may be no easy answer. The outcome of different actions may be unclear, and a principled decision may sometimes harm your beneficiaries.

One proactive remedy is personal determination and alertness to such challenges. Decide to keep an attentive attitude, and be ready to analyse difficult situations in the light of your principles and the norms you are committed to. You might have to stand up for them. This does not necessarily imply storming into the responsible minister's office to set him straight, but it does imply taking a stand.

When the challenge occurs, raise it with your colleagues and your line of command to ensure well-deliberated, conscientious decisions. And what if you disagree with your line of command? If you do, it is time to examine your personal responsibility.

In October 1998 Denis Halliday resigned as UN Humanitarian Coordinator for Iraq, in protest against the sanctions regime.

In February 2000, Hans von Sponeck, the next UN Humanitarian Coordinator and Deputy Secretary General for Iraq, and Jutta Burghard, head of the UN World Food Programme in Iraq, resigned for the same reason. Halliday and Von Sponeck later published an article calling the sanctions a violation of the Geneva conventions and other international law because they were causing the deaths of thousands of Iraqis (*Guardian*, 29 November 2001).

When it comes to serious ethical matters, we must all be able to stand up for our action or non-action, regardless of our superior's position.[16]

Conclusions

If you have prepared well for your mission, you will have:

1 made sure you have the professional and linguistic qualifications needed, and the maturity and strength required for your mission;
2 studied your job description, plans of action and strategies;
3 discussed your mission with your employer;
4 acquainted yourself with international instruments, norms and principles that pertain to your mission;
5 linked up with contacts with relevant knowledge/experience, at home and/or in the field;
6 got a grasp on local history, culture, ethnicity/religion and traditions;
7 committed yourself to matching enthusiasm with realism and taking failures in your stride;
8 committed yourself to be alert to ethical issues.

Notes

1 www.unfpa.org/women/docs/res_1325e.pdf.
2 For a good overview of key documents and developments, see the website of the International Coalition for the Responsibility to Protect: www.responsibilitytoprotect.org/index.php/publications.
3 www.responsibilitytoprotect.org/.
4 www.oecd.org/corruption/oecdantibriberyconvention.htm.
5 The number later increased to 18.
6 www.g7plus.org/new-deal-endorsement/.
7 www.osce.org/odihr/43675.
8 www.ifrc.org/who-we-are/vision-and-mission/the-seven-fundamental-principles/.
9 http://web.worldbank.org/WBSITE/EXTERNAL/EXTDEC/EXTRESEARCH/EXTWDRS/0,contentMDK:23252415~pagePK:478093~piPK:477627~theSitePK:477624,00.html.
10 www.oxforddictionaries.com/definition/english/culture.
11 A clear and simple presentation of this topic is found in UN Volunteers (2012).
12 In a peace-building context Richmond (2011:58) refers to culture[s] 'as the site of agency from which politics and the state emerge'.
13 The Central African Republic's President Samba-Panza expressed a similar view on the country's conflicts between Muslims and Christians in an Al Jazeera TV interview on 14 February 2014.
14 The first government of East Timor did not develop a constructive relationship with the Catholic Church, which became a powerful adversary.
15 A number of dilemmas and proactive measures related to aid distribution are presented in our 'do no harm' discussion on p. 148.
16 In June 2014 Slim, H. presented a draft book for discussion at Oxford University, with the provisional title 'Humanitarian Ethics; A Guide to the Morality of Aid in War and Disaster'.

References

Anderson, M. (1999) *Do No Harm: 'How Aid Can Support Peace – or War'*, Boulder, CO: Lynne Rienner.

DFID (undated) *Building Peaceful States and Societies. A DFID Practice Paper*, www.gsdrc.org/docs/open/CON75.pdf.

European Union (2007) *Code of Conduct on Complementarity and the Division of Labour in Development Policy*, http://europa.eu/legislation_summaries/development/general_development_framework/r13003_en.htm.

European Union (2009) *Concept on Strengthening EU Mediation and Dialogue Capacities*, http://eeas.europa.eu/cfsp/conflict_prevention/docs/concept_strengthening_eu_med_en.pdf.

G7+ (2011) *The New Deal*, www.g7plus.org/new-deal-document/.

Jansen, G. R. (1999) *Albanians and Serbs in Kosovo: An Abbreviated History: An Opening for the Islamic Jihad in Europe*, http://lamar.colostate.edu/~grjan/kosovohistory.html.

Lauffer, S., Degen-Heinemann, S. and Hamacher, J. (2013) *In Control. A Practical Guide for Civilian Experts Working in Crisis Management Missions*, http://ec.europa.eu/dgs/fpi/announcements/news/20130924_en.htm.

Narayan, G. (undated) *Children in Armed Conflict, Peacebuilding, Operational Framework*, CIDA, www.acdi-cida.gc.ca/INET/IMAGES.NSF/vLUImages/Childprotection/$file/E10.pdf.

Oberg, K. (1960) 'Culture shock: adjustment to new cultural environments', *Practical Anthropology* 7: 77–182.

OECD (2007) The Security Sector Reform handbook, www.oecd.org/development/incaf/38406485.pdf.

OECD, DAC (1999) *Guidelines for Gender Equality and Women's Empowerment in Development Cooperation*, www.oecd.org/dac/gender-development/dacguidelinesongenderequality.htm.

OECD, DAC (2011) *Supporting Statebuilding in Situations of Conflict and Fragility: Policy Guidance*, www.oecd-ilibrary.org/development/supporting-statebuilding-in-situations-of-conflict-and-fragility_9789264074989-en.

Ofstad, O. (2012) *Reconciliation and Conflict Resolution in East Timor. Lessons for Future Operations*, www.elac.ox.ac.uk/downloads/Reconciliation%20and %20conflict%20resoloution%20in%20East%20Timor%20Apr%202012.pdf.

OSCE (2005) *Human Dimension Commitments: Thematic Compilation,* Second edition, Volume 1, www.osce.org/odihr/elections/16363.

Papagianni, K. (2008) 'Participation and state legitimation', in C. Call with V. Wyeth (eds) *Building States to Build Peace*, Boulder, CO: Lynne Rienner.

Richmond, O.P. (2011) *A Post-Liberal Peace*. (Routledge Studies in Peace and Conflict Resolution), London and New York.

Storti C. (1994) *Cross-Cultural Dialogues: 74 Brief Encounters with Cultural Difference*, Boston: Intercultural Press.

UN Volunteers (2012) *Cultural Induction and Awareness Training*, www.unv.org/fileadmin/docdb/pdf/2012/Resources/Volunteer_Toolkit_Cultural_Induction_Awareness_training.pdf.

World Bank (2011) *The World Development Report*, http://web.worldbank.org/WBSITE/EXTERNAL/EXTDEC/EXTRESEARCH/EXTWDRS/0,,contentMDK:23252415~pagePK:478093~piPK:477627~theSitePK:477624,00.html.

3 Establishing yourself in the field

You have now arrived. If you have done your homework, you may have a fair understanding of the country's or region's history and culture, including its religion and ethnicity. If not, you will have to work on this in the field.

Lectures/seminars?

Unless your employer has planned for it, you will not have much time for studies. One possibility is to invite local resource personnel for a learning session. A lecture on culture by a local anthropologist may be very useful. So may discussions with historians, sociologists, economists, political scientists and lawyers. Local civil servants may also be eligible to give such briefings, as may village elders or religious leaders.

Perhaps you could get a group of such resource persons together for a seminar. If you explain that your wish is to be culturally sensitive and show respect to the local community, you are likely to get a positive response. If so, be prepared to arrange the seminar yourself or together with colleagues. If you organise sessions for subjects, such as history, local governance, culture and religion, and assign your local partners to do introductory presentations, you should be in business.

Just one piece of advice: you need to make sure that no resource person is associated with conflicts in ways that could harm your respect or integrity.

Defining your own role

Once all due preparations are completed, it is time to plan your work. How do you go about it? While many of your tasks may be given, others may be a question of imagination and initiative. To the extent that you have the freedom of choice, the issues will be: what can I do to contribute to the overriding goals of the mission? What is the optimal use of my resources? This may to a large extent be a question of straightforward implementation of your job description, but subject to the freedom you have, there may be different ways of approaching your work.

You might wish to develop your own personal strategy. If so, try to define:

- What concrete goals should I set for myself?
- What should my tasks be to achieve these?

Conflicts are also a relevant factor if you develop a personal strategy. To a large extent your position and your mission will decide whether you can exert direct influence on conflicts. You should in any case have a clear view on the conflicts that may influence achievement of your goals.

Do not underestimate the importance of how you, as a single individual, relate to conflicts. The efforts of one person may initiate important developments, positive or negative. The murder in Sarajevo that may have triggered the First World War is one dramatic example; the self-immolation in Tunisia that triggered the Arab Spring in 2010 is another. Less dramatic, a blunder by a international delegate may trigger negative reactions in a nervous population whereas his/her positive interaction with key actors could induce peaceful outcomes.

If active conflict management is beyond the scope of your work, meaning that your activities may only have an indirect effect on peace, you should at times revisit the account of Mary Anderson's book *Do no Harm* on p. 148.

Conflicts of significance

Chapter 6 on peacebuilding suggests that a comprehensive multi-sector conflict analysis should be the basis of peacebuilding plans. However, this kind of comprehensive analysis may never have been conducted. The UN's analyses are not the kind recommended in this book, and some are internal documents, only available to UN personnel (see p. 111).

In any case an overall analysis might not address in depth the conflicts you come across in your work. To the extent that there are conflicts of importance for your mission, you need to relate to them constructively. This means that you may have to conduct an analysis on your own or together with colleagues in the field. Advice on this subject is offered on p. 113. You should also relate constructively to conflicts in a programming context (pp. 144–148).

What kind of peace?

Apart from the absence of warfare, what does peace imply? We have observed our duty to observe human rights. What else do we need to observe?

Peacebuilding approaches and concepts have to a large extent been reflected western ideas of liberal democracy, meaning party-based parliamentarianism and markets open to free trade. You may go to work in countries with different traditions. There may never have been a parliament, and local leadership was perhaps handled by councils of elders or religious leaders. Rather than trade, farming and fishing may be the predominant basis of subsistence.

We often find that liberal peacebuilding approaches benefit political and economic elites who use new democratic conditions to pursue their own interests. Elected governments may centralise and grab as much power as they can, employing their supporters in all public positions and exploiting the country's resources. We find monopolies that make the elite richer and abuse the poor.

How can we help to ensure developments that are in the interest of the people? There is no simple answer to this, but we are obliged to ask the question.[1] If you hold a senior position involving high-level discussions or decision-making, it is your obligation to raise this issue with political leaders. What does fair peace mean in this country, and how can the peacebuilding process help the people achieve it? Comprehensive, inclusive political dialogue, involving people and stakeholders at all levels of society, may be needed. The winners of an armed conflict or the ruling elite may not want this, but we are obliged to keep the interests of the nation in mind. This may cause a difficult dilemma. Leading UN member countries have emphasised that peacebuilding must happen on the terms of the recipient country and must not be imposed by the international community,[2] and the New Deal (endorsed by 35 countries and six international organisations by January 2013) states that plans and vision must be country-led and country-owned. While this view is morally hard to oppose, we have a problem if the recipient state is synonymous with a group of people who are hijacking democracy for their own designs.

Democracy is widely regarded as a cornerstone in peacebuilding. Instead of support to democracy, this book advocates support to 'sound political development' (p. 120). This relates to the above concerns, including the fact that local governance traditions may not be commensurate with our ideas of party-based elections, and that time and consideration may be needed for the country in question to decide on its own direction.

If you work on a small project in some remote district, you may not feel this is your problem. We should, however, always be aware of the rings we spread, including what kind of peace we are contributing to. Our attitudes are therefore important.

Establishing local contacts

The knowledge you have acquired of the country/region, your mission and conflicts must, subject to your position, be followed up with practical action in the field.

Identifying important actors is part of this follow-up. In addition to parties to existing and threatened conflicts, there may be opinion leaders and other persons influencing the conflicts or your work. The group may include politicians and civil servants, ministers, mayors, religious leaders and chiefs of police, as well as representatives of political parties and organisations, military and semi-military groups, the media and civilian organisations. These actors might also be natural interlocutors/sources of information, so also may the local elders of tribes, NGO staff, peace activists and local scientists. Key persons and opinion leaders are not always easily visible. Do your best to get the real picture.

Follow up on the information you have brought from home. Try to get a good picture of any actor you might wish to cooperate with.

What kind of interaction?

Constructive conflict management normally requires direct contact/communication with the groups and persons involved in the conflict as well as the ones contributing to peacebuilding and humanitarian relief/development. Coordination is an important aspect of international assistance work, and contacts/mutual support also matter in terms of security.

Colleagues may give you valuable information on working conditions/establishment in the field, and you should provide the same to other newcomers.

Regular meetings

You would normally need regular meetings with partners and colleagues. Unless cooperation is established, you may need to take an initiative. If you have the authority to take such steps, invite other relevant agencies to a joint meeting and raise the question of broad-based constructive interaction.

Since the mandate of each organisation is hardly ever clear to everybody, a natural start may be to ask the representatives to explain their mandates and their views on the possibilities of cooperation and coordination. If you all agree to cooperate and how to do it, establish a meeting structure and routines that ensure continuity, such as weekly/biweekly meetings, and decide who is to host and chair them. For advice on coordination, see pp. 139–143.

Cooperation with security forces

Cooperating with military units, peacekeepers included, raises special concerns. Armed forces are meant to apply force or show the potential of force, whereas civilian agencies are not. Civilian actors in peace or humanitarian missions should in general avoid being associated with military forces. The Oslo Guidelines,[3] a document developed in 1992–1994 by 16 nations and a number of international organisations including UN agencies and the EU, offers guidance for humanitarian cooperation with military forces. A main point is that humanitarian needs should if possible be met by humanitarian organisations and not the army. However, humanitarian needs often exceed the capacity of civilian organisations, and in some countries the army is the biggest humanitarian actor. UN peacekeeping forces may also occasionally conduct humanitarian work. In both cases some degree of cooperation may be appropriate. Your organisation may have its own guidelines or instructions on this subject. If not, you should discuss the subject with your reporting line.

It may be natural and useful to attend joint meetings and coordinate efforts, both with UN forces and the national army. However, if you visit an army unit that is viewed with fear and contempt, you may invite suspicion, and you should not operate with it in the field. So if you and an army unit are addressing needs in the same village, you should avoid being seen together.[4]

Sometimes the security situation prevents safe travel, and a military escort is essential. If you choose to accept this escort, be aware that it may affect people's perceptions of your agency. The same pertains to police escort. Apart from the risk of being associated with security forces, such an escort signals that 'we do not feel safe here', something that might create distance between you and the people. Joining a generally respected UN force in the field may seem less problematic, but such respect does not always last in volatile environments.

Inviting outsiders to cooperation meetings

Sometimes it may be wise to invite representatives of the local administration or opinion leaders to cooperation/coordination meetings. Let them see that you are doing your best to support the local society and that you also support each other. (Remember, unity strengthens.) Let them forward their own proposals or points of view and invite discussion. This may encourage a feeling of shared responsibility and identify potential partners. Your organisation may perhaps be in a position to accommodate a wish, say, for provisions to a vulnerable village that has fallen off the radar of the international community. Others may undertake to repair a road or a grenade-damaged school. Such responses to local wishes may boost the reputation of the international community and facilitate work.

Observe your mandate

Occasionally the desire for cooperation may clash with your mandate. For example: the UNHCR or OSCE desires your presence at a meeting with the local mayor, aimed at discussing the problem of house reconstruction being stalled by corruption. This is beyond your mandate, but you are concerned with the people's housing situation and winter is nearing. What do you do?

Obviously one has to abide by one's own mandate, and you may sometimes have to clarify with your superiors where to draw the line. Remember, though, that representatives of international organisations may sometimes make a contribution through their sheer presence. In the above-mentioned meeting with the mayor, a delegate from a respected organisation participating as an observer may contribute to an atmosphere of seriousness, even if she refrains from any active participation.

Contact with local authorities

A good rapport with local authorities may determine your organisation's success. You may come to need the goodwill and cooperation of local authorities, not just in your efforts for peace but also for security reasons. The authorities' attitude towards international organisations will also influence the attitudes of the local population, of opinion leaders and of other resource persons. It is therefore highly important that you make the contacts you need. How do you do it?

Confidence-building/courtesy calls

There is nothing better than a courtesy call to establish contact and create a constructive atmosphere. Such calls are signals of respect and address an important human need. An omission may be perceived as offensive and could in the worst case have dangerous consequences. It is better to make one too many visits than one too few. If you are to relate to a conflict, your need to be respected and seen as impartial requires that you should visit all parties. Therefore, find out whom to visit, and do it.

Courtesy calls range from a pleasant meeting with a new colleague in a cooperating organisation to visiting an unpredictable warlord who is sternly against the presence of international organisations. The first situation demands very little. The following advice addresses the more demanding visit.

The first meeting

Ring, write or send a message to get an appointment. Make it clear that it is a courtesy call you want, nothing else. This enhances your chances of a positive reception.

Note that the first meeting may be decisive for the interaction that will follow since the frames are being set at this stage. Be careful about your approach. The meeting should facilitate confidence-building and the establishment of your role. Most of us will strike a cordial tone from the start, but international personnel are sometimes so concerned with gaining respect that they forget this.

Start the conversation with something harmless. Introduce yourself and your organisation, and describe your mandate and the work you are planning to do. An overview is normally enough. Explain that you seek positive interaction with important groups and persons in the local community, and if you are dealing with conflicts, that you wish to meet persons from both or all sides. In addition to impartiality and respectability, this may also indicate authority.

A positive approach is to ask your host for his view on subjects of mutual interest, such as development in the area, security, his group's situation, etc. You may hear statements that deviate considerably from what you consider to be the truth.

In the first meeting, we would all like to give a positive impression of ourselves, our own organisation or group. You may for instance hear a leader of a paramilitary group with a dubious reputation state that he is concerned with everybody's security. If so, what is your response? Don't protest. You will present your view later, in a different way. (See pp. 62–63 on how such statements can be used in a positive way.) The point here and now is to start developing the relationship you wish, be it cooperation or simply the acceptance of your organisation's presence and work.

Express understanding for your host's view as far as you can without compromising yourself. Identify points of agreement and emphasise them.

During the first meeting refrain from raising conflicts and subjects that imply criticism, unless you absolutely have to. It may spur a defensive attitude and perhaps aggression, reactions that could be difficult to deal with later. If you cannot avoid voicing criticism in this meeting, see p. 86 on ways of doing it.

Authority/credibility/expertise

These factors are of general significance. The respect you manage to gain will influence all interaction and may be decisive the day a crisis occurs. Authority pertains to who you are, whom you represent and the impression you give. Credibility demands clarity and firmness when you describe your mission. Do not hesitate to refer to the underlying principles of your mandate. Expertise indicating that you are well qualified for your mission will strengthen your position and should normally be revealed, but in a discreet way. For further information on these factors see pp. 76–77.

Friendliness and humour

The chances of acceptance and an understanding of your mission will be greatly helped by a friendly approach. Authority may be combined with both friendliness and humour, which can be valuable icebreakers.

What kind of interaction?

At an early stage it may be difficult to assess what kind of interaction or cooperation is appropriate. Sometimes it is clear that cooperation is out of the question, but you may still need your counterpart's goodwill to carry out your work. Respect and politeness are then keywords, as is information.

One possibility is to offer to get in touch either regularly or when something particularly interesting happens in your field. (Even with strict professional secrecy you would normally find something that could be communicated.) Alternatively, if nothing impedes it, suggest a visit to your office for a cup of coffee and maybe an introduction to your colleagues. Such an approach appeals to most people.

Concluding the meeting

Try to get an appointment for an early follow-up meeting if this is a person you need to maintain contact with. Establishing contact should in general be followed up as early as possible. When concluding the meeting, take the opportunity to consolidate the essence of your agreement or understanding. A brief summing up, combined with a firm handshake and eye contact, is recommended. The objective is that when the meeting is over, you are to leave the following impression:

- You are a likeable person and someone it will be nice to meet again.
- You are credible and induce respect and authority.

- You stand for values and principles without being judgemental.
- You show basic respect for other human beings.
- You expect cooperation or positive interaction.
- You may have initiated an element of friendship (which in general makes reciprocal services and affirmations natural). Some might react negatively to the idea of being friendly with persons of dubious qualities or reputation. It is important to observe, however, that this does not imply social interaction or acceptance of persons' acts or attitudes. See 'The element of friendship', pp. 79–80.

When someone refuses to meet you

This is not a rare occurrence. It often materialises as non-availability. The person in question is either 'not present' or 'busy' and never returns your calls. The reasons may be repugnance towards the international presence, your organisation or even you or your predecessor personally. It could also happen that you or your unit are not considered important enough. This may be a difficult challenge. If you don't expect the reluctant person to become important for your work, you might be better off ignoring him. If he is important, you should not give in without further efforts.

How to obtain a meeting

One possibility may be to use contacts. If the person in question is a civil servant, you may perhaps gain access to him via other civil servants or public bodies. It may also be worth trying to involve his superiors or representatives of other parts of public administration. Other organisations or persons might also be willing to take an initiative. If you are in contact with your embassy, you might perhaps get some support there. Some would go as far as turning up at places the person visits and try to make direct contact. Examples may include everything from seminars and meetings to garden parties. The point is to find the opportunity to introduce yourself and establish a first contact. If you try this approach, do it with subtlety.

It may also be an option to contact the person directly in his or her office. Here, too, subtlety is required. If, despite all your efforts, someone makes himself unavailable, you may opt to give up. In the worst case your protracted efforts may appear as self-humiliation, something that hardly serves your mission.

Meeting with negative persons

If you manage to establish contact with a negative counterpart, the challenge will be to influence him sufficiently for a positive interaction to take place. The rules of courtesy calls also apply here. Additionally, a negative counterpart will often present challenges such as aggression and negative criticism. This requires tact. The basic rule is not to respond in the same manner. Polarisation normally excludes cooperation and further contact. Your first signal should be that you are a pleasant, balanced and confident person.

Ignore possible offences and show that you want a serious talk. Listen actively and show that you are listening. (See 'Empathy and active listening' on p. 71). Find out if there is anything on which you can express understanding or agreement. If your counterpart's criticism is justified, express support. This is likely to dampen negative emotions and pave the way for a more relaxed tone. If you have to express deviating points of view, don't call them disagreements. The point is not only to show respect, understanding and interest, but also to earn respect and to make yourself an interesting counterpart. If you achieve this, possibilities will open up.

Use of interpreters

Most international missions depend on interpreters, for introductory meetings as well as negotiations. An important element when establishing yourself in the field is therefore to ensure access to well-qualified interpreters.

Employment

You should subject candidates to a thorough language test, both written and verbal. If English is your working language, arrange a test with exact *ad verbum* translation, for instance with the aid of an employee who has command of both the local language and English. Another way to gauge the candidate's language skills is to give her an English text that she is to translate verbally into the local language. The translation should be taped and replayed to an already employed, skilled interpreter who then translates the text into English.

Make the following clear to the candidate

- Only strict *ad verbum* translation is accepted, with no changes, summaries or explanations to your counterparts. Exceptions are accepted if you commit a serious cultural blunder and the interpreter saves you, in which case you are to be informed as soon as possible. The interpreter must also inform you about obscurities or ambiguities that render the translation unclear.
- No disloyalty will be tolerated. Beware that some interpreters serving international organisations are debriefed regularly by local authorities/intelligence agencies.

Communication

- Remember to speak in short sentences, with pauses so that the interpreter can follow you. You may need to suggest the same to counterparts who are not used to with interpreters.
- Look at your counterpart, not the interpreter.

- Use two alternating interpreters for long meetings. If your counterpart brings her own interpreter, each may translate for her party separately. If you have someone present who speaks the local language without functioning as interpreter, you should inform your counterpart. This is a matter of trust.
- Remember that communication with interpreters takes time.

Conclusions

If you are well established in the field, you will have:

1 developed further the knowledge you brought from home, possibly using local resource persons;
2 gained a good understanding of existing and potential conflicts;
3 decided on the need for a personal strategy, and possibly developed one;
4 established contacts that are appropriate for your work;
5 initiated positive interaction with strategically important persons, groups and organisations;
6 made sure you have good interpreters.

Notes

1 A profound discussion of such aspects is offered by Richmond (2011).
2 See Gheciu and Welsh (2009).
3 http://reliefweb.int/sites/reliefweb.int/files/resources/8706B7B69BD77E00C1257233004F0570-OCHA-Nov2006.pdf.
4 For a discussion of interaction with military forces in armed conflict, see Jæger (2009).

References

Anderson, M. (1999) *Do No Harm: How Aid Can Support Peace – or War*, London: Lynne Rienner.

Gheciu, A. and Welsh, J. (2009) 'The imperative to rebuild: assessing the normative case for post conflict reconstruction', *Ethics & International Affairs* 23(2): 121–146.

Jæger, T. (2009) 'Humanitarian and military action in armed conflict: side by side, not hand in hand', *Nordic Journal of International Law* 78: 567–579.

Richmond, O.P. (2011) *A Post-Liberal Peace*. (Routledge Studies in Peace and Conflict Resolution), London and New York: Routledge.

Zaum, D. (2007) *The Sovereignty Paradox: The Norms and Politics of International Statebuilding*, New York: Oxford University Press.

4 Mediation

If the parties to a conflict desire a solution or a positive transformation, your challenge may be to facilitate a dialogue between them or possibly to initiate mediation. If the antagonism is too strong, your only possibility may be to intervene vis-à-vis one party or each party separately, and perhaps make active use of psychological influencing techniques. Such techniques may also play a role in mediation contexts, but you have much wider scope for applying them when alone with one party. These techniques are therefore dealt with in Chapter 5.

Facilitation

Facilitation is a keyword in conflict management. It implies that communication between the parties is being supported or rendered possible by a third party. This may happen in different ways. Statements or suggestions may be conveyed. Meetings between the parties may be arranged, and the parties may be assisted during negotiations. The parties themselves should, as far as possible, take responsibility for solving or transforming the conflict positively. This should be an objective for any facilitation or mediation.

Facilitation happens most frequently in meetings. Your challenge as a third party will be to contribute to the best possible process. This normally means helping the parties to clarify positions and interests, and relate to emotions, gain insight and understanding and engage in a constructive dialogue.

The mediation process

Mediation is a structured facilitation process, where two or more parties to a conflict receive assistance from a third to carry out discussions with a view to identifying positive solutions or changes. A mediator has no mandate to make decisions unless this is specifically agreed. Her mission is to contribute to constructive discussions within agreed frames. The role of a mediator demands impartiality and often neutrality, although, as indicated above, the crucial issue may be whether the mediator is trusted to conduct the role with fairness and integrity.

The mediator's task normally includes preparations for discussion. Frequently the mediator is also asked to follow up to ensure the implementation of agreements. Mediation is future-oriented, in the sense that solutions for the future are sought.

'Mediation light'

Occasionally the parties are not ready to seek solutions through meditation, but might accept to get together for a facilitated joint analysis of their conflict. If so, improved understanding of the conflict is the goal. Some conflict theorists reserve the term problem-solving for this particular process, which may indeed be a useful transformation tool. For our purpose we shall not discuss this tool separately, as the techniques described in this chapter will enable you to facilitate such a process, should the parties prefer this.

Preparations

In real life only a minority of international personnel come to act as mediators in a formalised, structured way. However, if you have knowledge of how such a process may be run, you will benefit in less formal mediations and negotiations. In tense and complex negotiations, structure and order may, however, be essential. Therefore, if asked to act as mediator, do yourself the favour of revisiting this chapter before you embark on the task, so that you have a clear picture of what you need to do.

So let us assume you are relating to a conflict that requires proper mediation. You have made sure that the parties want or at least accept mediation, and that you are accepted and preferably wanted in the role of mediator. Make sure you know the conflict well.

Parties, stakeholders and interests

You have to know the real parties and stakeholders, and which groups or forces are behind them, and to make sure it is the 'right' parties that meet. You must also know:

- Who will consider themselves affected by the negotiations?
- Who may block implementation?
- Whose approval will be needed?

The real interests have to be represented by real parties, none of whom should be excluded. If there are many parties, it may be necessary to split the mediation into several processes. If negotiators are claiming to represent parties, you may ask for signed authorisation.

Try to find out as much as possible about the parties and their background. Do you know the parties' interests? Unless this is a familiar subject to you, revisit pp. 4–5. Remember that a position in itself often does not reveal interests. Can you identify basic human needs that might be threatened? You will find that an essential part of the mediation process depicted in this chapter involves identifying and meeting the parties' interests, but it is useful to have a best possible picture before you start working with the parties. So start looking into this at an early stage.

What is the purpose of the mediation?

This has to be cleared with the parties. Is it to find a solution, subdue antagonism or prevent escalation? Should one limit the discussions to parts of the conflict? If looking at the Indian/Pakistani conflict on Kashmir, it would today be a heavy task to mediate on Kashmir's status. Experience has showed that a number of single aspects may be negotiated with a view to reducing the total pressure. Examples are border traffic, trade and communication.[1]

Meeting the parties separately

It is a common misunderstanding that if we can only get adversaries to talk, we are on the way to something positive. The fact is that deep conflicts are normally marked by mutual mistrust.

Even if the parties wish to resolve their conflict, the idea of sitting down with the opponent to discuss it may be repulsive. And strong emotional outbursts and confrontations might worsen the antagonism. The parties should therefore not meet before you believe that they can have a constructive interaction. To get there, a series of bilateral meetings might be required.

You may find that discriminating between person and case is a problem. The difference between position and interests may also need clarification, and the different layers of interest may be even more difficult to understand.

Discuss these concepts with the parties and help them clarify their thoughts. It might help to show them an example of a chain of interests such as the one outlined on p. 5. Since they have accepted mediation, the parties will normally have an interest in resolving the conflict. What other interests do they have?

You might also discuss the opponents' positions with each of them. Make sure they understand what the opponent wants and if possible why he wants it. Invite the parties to explore what the opponent's interests might be. If you succeed in creating mutual understanding for underlying interests and perhaps basic needs, the chances of a constructive mediation process will increase.

Your assistance might include:

- asking questions;
- rephrasing unclear or aggressive statements;
- organising speech and thoughts into clear messages;
- extracting main points and principles.[2]

Do your best to ensure that the parties are capable of communicating appropriately with each other. One revealing question might be how they think their counterpart should behave in the mediation process. Do they demand civil, constructive communication, or are accusations and aggression acceptable? The purpose of this question is the mirror effect, making each party realise the need to contribute to a constructive climate.

Sometimes mediators find themselves positioned as a go-between for quite some time before the parties are ready to meet. Unless it is a matter of urgency you should take the time needed to ensure constructive interaction.[3]

Practical advice

We now presume the parties are ready to negotiate, or you may have found that negotiations cannot wait.

- Send a written invitation or confirmation with a clear indication of the subjects under discussion and practical information of significance.
- Make sure the parties will come. Written confirmation is desirable, but often hard to get.
- Ensure the settings are practically and formally appropriate. The venue must be ample and comfortable. It must be safe, quiet and appropriate as to space and light.
- Provide coffee, tea and other refreshments.
- If possible, avoid having the parties sit opposite each other. A round table is recommended.
- There should be rooms for separate discussions.
- Provide a secretary to take minutes and a well-qualified interpreter, two if the meeting is expected to be long.
- Security aspects should be observed. Is it necessary to have guards, protect and escort the delegates, or prepare for possible emergency evacuation?
- Depending on your mandate, you may need to make sure that you can communicate with your superiors.

Introductory phase

Start by welcoming the parties. Make sure everybody is properly introduced. Include some small talk, perhaps also humour to lighten the atmosphere.

In the capacity of mediator you will normally offer to be chairperson, but the parties should give their acceptance as this commits them to respect. In the following we assume that you are functioning as both the chairperson and the mediator.

Frames

Goal

All negotiation processes should have a goal, meaning a specific purpose (see below). It is desirable for the parties to agree on a joint statement of goals. This may prevent disagreement later on.

Strategy

You should raise with the parties whether it is relevant to agree on a strategy for the process. The strategic approach recommended here is:

1 the parties' presentation
2 clarifying the problem
3 identifying interests
4 finding ways of meeting the interests
5 seeking solutions
6 drawing up an agreement
7 following up on the agreement.

If there are problems discussing strategy at an early stage, this may be deferred till after the contents of the conflict have been discussed. For conflicts consisting of only one simple subject, a strategy is normally not needed.

Meeting plan

If the conflict is comprehensive, you may wish to agree on a schedule. The first meeting may contain presentations and clarification of the problem, the second an identification of the parties' interests etc. If there are several conflict issues, a parallel process (pp. 51–52) is normally recommended. You may also wish to agree that the meetings are to be concluded by a certain date, to give the parties an inducement to follow up.

Meeting agenda

Each meeting should have a purpose and an agenda. When agreeing on an agenda, make sure you set aside abundant time for all items, be it a discussion of strategy, rules of order, the parties' presentations, breaks, summing up, etc. Do not overload the agenda. It is very unfortunate if the meeting fails because of time constraints.

'Traffic rules'

Rules of order must be established, including respect for allotted speaking time and a ban on interruptions, offensive language and possible taboo subjects. The chairperson's authority to crack down on breaches of rules must be agreed upon. Emphasise that your participation depends on respect for the rules. One may agree on sanctions, but this is a sensitive issue. Ask for the parties' explicit endorsement of the rules to ensure their commitment.

Minutes

The parties should decide what to include in the minutes, which normally means all agreements of significance. The minutes should be in your organisation's working language, but translation to a local version may be required.

The parties' presentations

Start by very briefly outlining the problem as you perceive it. Then give the floor to the parties one by one to present their positions. Drawing lots on who is to start may be required. Agree on speaking time.

To encourage dialogue, request the parties to speak directly to each other. Some suggest they should speak to the chairperson instead, so as to feel free to express themselves. The danger is that this makes it easier to accuse and offend the other party. Emphasise the ban on interruptions.

Remember that as chairperson you must crack down on violations of the agreed rules. A meeting that degenerates may worsen the conflict. In the event of violations such as offensive language, interruptions or statements on taboo subjects, you must immediately stop the proceedings and demand respect for the rules. You might express your understanding of the conflict as being an emotional one, but stress that order and reciprocal respect are a precondition for your participation. In the worst case you must consider withdrawing as mediator, but give the parties a chance to get back on track.

Even if you have helped the parties clarify their positions, interests and needs in preparatory meetings, you should be prepared to do it again when they make their presentations. Make sure you render all such assistance in a tactful way, particularly if you have to interrupt.

After each presentation you should sum up the party's points of view and get confirmation. Choose your wording carefully with a view to softening antagonism. You should normally not take minutes here. Disagreement should not be cemented.

Emotions

Putting emotions into words may provide a useful release of tension and sometimes may contribute to mutual understanding. There is, however, often a risk of uncontrolled outbursts and it may be better to allow venting of feelings only in separate meetings with the mediator. You may also suggest deferring possible emotional input till a calmer stage has been reached, and you are confident that the parties are reasonable enough. As long as tension is high, expression of emotions should be banned.[4] If you decide to invite venting of feelings, the parties may avoid accusations if you help them link their feelings to the needs that prompted them.

Clarifying the problem

Agreeing/disagreeing

This phase starts with establishing what the parties agree on. Have the parties help you with the process. Emphasise all points of agreement and list them on a flip-chart. Hang the chart on the wall for reference. Any identified agreement is a psychological advantage. The more agreement between the parties, the easier the continuation. (On this subject see p. 74.) Give praise for all agreements the parties identify.

Establish together with the parties which problems are unsolved. Here too a flip-chart is recommended. List the parties' deviating positions. Help them clarify what have been the biggest obstacles to solution or positive change. This may sometimes identify 'shortcuts' to a solution.

Having cleared the parties' positions it may be useful if, together with them, you *establish what is likely to happen if the negotiations fail*. The seriousness and importance of succeeding will thus become part of the background. It is, however, important not to overestimate the extent of the problems. This may reinforce a negative focus, and your task is to induce positive cooperation.

Avoiding negative focus

Parties to a conflict may be inclined to focus solely on negative aspects, particularly in case of escalation or if the conflict is longstanding. They may easily disregard whatever is positive or functions well between them, thinking 'we have a conflict' as if it were a constant factor, even if in reality it poses a problem only occasionally,[5] as in this instance:

> Two villages have a conflict over the right to a well. A close look at the issue may reveal that the problem emerges only during periods of drought, and that people from the two villages otherwise interact without negative incidents. If so, focusing on this may give them a more realistic and less negative picture. This may enhance their possibilities of a cooperative approach.

After identification of the issues of disagreement, it may be worth asking:

- When do you not experience the conflict?
- What is it like then?
- What do the parties do then?

Shortcuts to a solution

If the parties identify clear and positive exceptions to the conflict situation, this may reveal opportunities for a shortcut to a solution or positive change. Discuss with the parties whether it is possible to repeat or expand the exceptions. Brief therapy psychologists working on family conflicts recommend that if something works, do more of it. This approach may also be applied to other conflicts. Examples:

> Two countries in a border dispute have had a peaceful period when the borders were completely open and peaceful cross-border trade flourished. The border issue itself was at that stage less significant. Could this exception be explored as a basis for positive transformation?

> Two ethnic groups in conflict function well together in some contexts. They trade peacefully, cooperate on sports events, and women's organisations from each side enjoy good relationships. Is it possible to expand and develop these activities, and to copy them in other contexts?

Even if such approaches do not resolve the conflict, they may have the effect of improving the relationship between the parties.

Similarly, focusing on what has kept the parties from resolving their conflict may sometimes help identify shortcuts to resolution. If such possibilities are identified early on, the parties may wish to pursue them on the spot and drop other efforts. If the quest for a shortcut does not succeed, you can always help the parties get back on track later. You may also resume the 'shortcut' approach when you get to the resolution phase (p. 49). As chairperson, you should be aware of potential shortcuts at all times. The question 'Can we do it like this?' sometimes turns out to be magic.

Identifying interests

Unless the parties succeed in finding shortcuts to a solution, the next step after the parties' presentations is to address their interests.

A point-by-point process

Raise the issues of disagreement one by one, using the positions as headings on flip-charts.

The parties should now be requested to describe the interests underlying their positions. Remember also at this stage to agree on a time limit on arguments. Under each position, note the party's interests layer by layer.

You have probably been through this already in separate meetings with the parties, but do not be surprised if they still find it difficult to discriminate between interests and positions. The parties sometimes tend to simply repeat their presentations, and your active guidance may be needed.

One reason why interests are sometimes hard to detect, is that they are overshadowed by antagonism. As previously observed, the situation that led to the conflict may also have changed. As a mediator, you have to help clarify this; you have to help the parties identify the interests that are relevant today.

Let us assume that two parties have longstanding conflict over a piece of land. When the problem arose, they both needed the land for agriculture and survival. If they both later acquired other land, their original needs might now be covered. The conflict may, however, persist. Perhaps bitterness or habit is keeping it alive? Maybe other needs have emerged in the meantime? Could it be that respect and understanding from the other party are what is needed today? If so, a scheme for reconciliation may be the answer.

As observed above, a party may have a number of different interests underlying her position. Her desire to own a property may derive from a wish to grow vegetables as well as a desire to build a house and get access to a well that provides potable water. If so, it may facilitate the process if you ask her to prioritise her interests, listing them as numbers 1, 2 and 3. The idea is to keep track of what is most important when you start identifying possible resolutions later on.

Basic needs

If an atmosphere of cooperation is established, you may agree with the parties to try to go all the way down to basic human needs. You have probably addressed these issues in separate meetings, but adversaries rarely find it easy to present their basic needs to each other.

Provided they are willing, continue on the chart where you have listed the positions and interests and explore together what needs may lie underneath. Don't be critical of the parties' suggestions. Try to include all levels or 'layers'. Occasionally the parties have more than one chain of interests, in which case you may need several charts.

Involve the parties as actively as possible in the process. Ask: 'What needs might underlie your counterpart's position?' Identifying an opponent's needs evokes empathy. You may also conduct this process as a brainstorming session (p. 51) if the parties agree. Hang the parties' charts up beside each other. The process has the following advantages:

- Alternative ways of meeting interests may emerge at all levels.
- It becomes easier to develop mutual understanding, since we all recognise important human needs.

So how does this work in practice?

Table 4.1 Conflict between town A and town B: chain of interests

Town A	*Town B*
Position: To own property **Interests:** 1 To build a cultural centre 2 To arrange exhibitions and shows 3 To make one's own culture known to others Basic needs: identity and respect	**Position:** To own property **Interests:** 1 To access a water well 2 To ensure pure drinking water Basic needs: health and survival

Let us use the example on pp. 4–5 and imagine two towns in conflict over a property. One party wants it to build a cultural centre. The other wants it because it has a good water well. The result might be two flip-charts looking like those in Table 4.1.

Unless joint ownership of the property is an option, both parties' positions cannot be met, and we have to explore whether their interests can.

Ways to meet interests

Invite the parties to suggest possible ways of meeting the identified interests layer by layer, but your discreet indication of possibilities will probably be required. The mediator should handle the writing at this stage. To avoid putting pressure on the parties, all possibilities should be noted as questions. The outcome depends on the parties' and your imagination, but you might get two flip-charts similar to those shown in Table 4.2.

Table 4.2 Conflict between town A and town B: ways of meeting interests

Town A	*Town B*
Interest 1: To build a cultural centre • Will B's access to the well obstruct plans for a cultural centre? • Would a pipeline avoid obstruction? • Could a centre be built elsewhere?	**Interest 1: Access to a well** • Will a cultural centre obstruct B's access to the well? • Is a pipeline from the well an option? • Are there alternative wells?
Interest 2: Exhibitions and shows • Does the town have other appropriate buildings available? • Could localities be rented or bought? **Interest 3: To make one's own culture known** • Are there other ways of making A's culture known to others?	**Interest 2: Pure drinking water** • Could B connect to a public water pipe in the vicinity? • Is water harvesting an option? • Could a purification plant elsewhere meet the need?
Basic needs: identity and respect • Could A's need for respect and identity be met in other ways? (A sensitive question that requires caution.)	**Basic needs: health and survival** • (As these needs depend on pure water, they cannot be met in other ways.)

You encourage the parties to discuss all options that seem interesting. In doing so, you may use separate flip-charts for each possible solution so as to explore it more in detail. As you proceed, each party should ask himself:

- What can I do and what do I have that may meet my counterpart's interests?
- What can they do and what do they have that may meet mine?

Any action, asset, value, property, right or concession could, in principle, be relevant.[6]

The parties may not be very keen to indicate their contributions. Try to make them understand that identifying possibilities does not commit them to anything, and that solutions will be discussed later. If necessary, take a break for internal discussions.

Let us imagine that the above parties find that a pipe from the well to town B would not obstruct a cultural centre. What if A has a stock of surplus pipes?

Let us also imagine that we explore alternative ways of making A's culture known to the world. What if B has a director of culture known for her creativity, who could come and work with A on their needs?

A good brainstorming session (see p. 51) might sometimes reveal surprising possibilities.

Can the cake be expanded?

It may pay to ask: is there anything both parties could contribute beyond the issue of conflict? Imagination used this way sometimes reveals unexpected options.

Let us say that village B has had a food shortage due to drought, while A has a good emergency stock of rice-seed. Assistance to B with this problem might contribute to a solution to the land issue, even if it has nothing to do with the conflict. Or let us say that A does not have a proper bulldozer to construct a much needed road through some rugged terrain, while B has one. Assistance to A in this could also help solve the land conflict.

If you go beyond the conflict issue in this way, you must make sure the parties agree on a balanced approach. No one should be allowed to blackmail a counterpart who is in serious need.

Seeking solutions

Once the possibilities of meeting the parties' interests and needs have been discussed and clarified, it is time to seek solutions or positive change. Perhaps some identified alternative offers an obvious solution, but this is not usually the case.

Ask the parties to study the possibilities they have identified, and encourage them to come forward with any suggestion they can think of, such as:

- solutions
- steps towards solutions
- measures that may induce positive developments.

They may need to be given time, maybe until the next meeting, to ponder the issue.

Relevant questions

When requesting proposals from the parties, you might ask: what could you possibly suggest that your counterpart might accept? Brief therapy psychologists sometimes address conflicts with a so-called miracle question: 'Imagine that you wake up tomorrow and the problem is solved. What is it like then? What do the parties do?'

The idea is both to help the parties adopt a positive focus and to identify possible solutions. The same question may be worth raising in mediation. But if you do, remember to emphasise that the solution should be a 'miracle' to both parties.

Unless this approach leads to a real miracle, you will have to ask a number of more targeted questions, some of which may go beyond the scope of interest-based solutions:

- Is it possible to find solutions that meet both parties' positions? (This might have been excluded early on, but you may revisit the issue when exploring solutions.)
- Is it possible to meet both parties' interests?
- Can you identify combinations of interest coverage?[7]
- Can you expand the cake?
- Can the parties repeat or expand exceptions from the conflict situation?
- If anything functions well between the parties, can this be built upon?
- Can one or both parties give or renounce something of less importance? A renunciation that is insignificant to one party could mean a lot to the other.
- If there are several conflict issues, can the parties trade values or concessions between the different issues? (See 'How do you run a parallel process?', pp. 51–52.)
- Can the parties agree to use objective criteria (see p. 53)?
- Can the parties agree on a solution technique (see p. 53)?

Concrete proposals for a solution from you as a mediator are only advisable if expressly agreed by the parties and may be sensitive vis-à-vis impartiality and neutrality.

Your task is to help the parties develop the process, so that they feel ownership of the outcome. Still, in one particular context you might wish to be assertive: you should help the parties avoid unrealistic solutions. Agreements that don't hold may lead to mutual blame and worsen their relationship. Small 'safe' steps of progress are normally better than big ones with a high risk of failing.[8]

Advice about the process

Brainstorming

If the atmosphere is good enough, a joint brainstorming session might be part of the process towards a solution. Invite the parties to put forward whatever proposals or ideas they can think of, based on free association. All proposals or ideas should be noted consecutively, without criticism or censorship of any kind, unless they are offensive. Again use a flip-chart.

Go through all the noted points with the parties. Everything found to be useless should be discarded. The rest should be taken up for discussion. Remember to highlight positive ideas, reactions and attitudes. Make these visible to both parties. Explicitly establish everything that indicates progress or possibilities.

The simplest first

The usual method is to start with the general and move to the particular. It is, however, very important that the parties enter a process where they find solutions and make progress. Therefore you should first address subjects where agreement seems within reach.

Break up complex conflicts

Some large conflicts consist of many small ones. If so, they should be split up to make them manageable. But this does not mean you should process them in isolation from each other.

Several problems in parallel

Research indicates that where there are several conflict issues between the same parties, it normally pays to run parallel processes (Pruitt and Rubin, 1986). This gives the parties access to a wider variety of possible concessions and ways to cover needs, and thus more combinations to draw on. The same pertains to situations where the parties have two totally different conflicts. It may be wise to establish that no agreement may be concluded until all problems have been solved. This is because an agreement will prevent the parties from going back to consider new combinations if they get stuck later on.[9]

How do you run a parallel process?

One way is to start with one subject of conflict, as we have suggested above, and work on it as far as possible. Then address the next subject in a similar process. As this process comes to an end, help the parties to identify points in the two subjects of conflict where it is possible to make exchanges. Explore whether offering a concession in one subject area can be met with a coherent step forward in the other. This may render new possibilities for progress.

You should get two sets of flip-charts and switch between them. Note down the possibilities that appear on a separate chart. But it is imperative that you are in control of the process at all times. Do not use this method if you find it too complicated.

Separate discussions with the parties?

Give the parties the possibility of withdrawing for internal discussions at any time. Sometimes a party might request a separate one-on-one session with the mediator to clarify issues of concern. Accept this if the parties agree and their confidence in you is not at stake.

Forms of resolution

Interest-based

Focusing on underlying needs may lead to the recognition that the parties have different, but adaptable interests.

This may reveal so-called win-win solutions. A well-known example from the international arena is the Sinai peninsula conflict between Israel and Egypt. Their positions pertained to conflicting claims to the area. The Camp David process in 1978 clarified that while the essential point for Egypt was to repossess lost land, Israel's interest was to avoid Egyptian military installations close enough to threaten its security. The solution identified through the process was that Egypt got back the land, but agreed to make it a demilitarised zone. This meant a win-win solution, in the sense that it met both parties' most important interests.

Once the parties' real interests have been identified, win-win solutions are sometimes easier to find than we expect. A much used exercise in conflict management training is to identify different ways of sharing an orange. Clearly there is no need to fight over the orange if one party wants the juice and the other wants the peel as a dish ingredient.

Position-based

Exceptionally, both parties' positions may be fully met, but for a position-based solution, reciprocal concessions are normally needed. If so, we have a compromise.

Compromise

A common misunderstanding is that the solution to a conflict has to imply compromise, meaning that both parties have to give up part of their claim. Sharing benefits or difficulties is typical of compromise. In the Egypt–Israel conflict, compromise might have meant dividing the area, which would have been a bad solution for both parties. Compromise may be a good solution if the parties find it acceptable to meet halfway, but it is normally worse than interest-based solutions.

Objective criteria

The parties may agree to seek solutions through objective criteria, such as 'What does the law say?' and 'What is decided in the peace agreement?' In the cases where needs-based solutions cannot be identified, this may be a constructive approach.[10]

Agreement on solution technique

It is sometimes practical to use solution techniques like arbitration[11] or drawing lots. Such techniques may be particularly appropriate if there are only two possible solutions.

Reconciliation

We have defined reconciliation as an interest-based process of change towards peace and harmony, although the relevant interests are usually different from those that originally caused the conflict. While we do not define reconciliation as conflict resolution, it is mentioned here as a process that is often needed to supplement conflict resolution.[12]

Expanded scope

Let us assume the parties have found a solution, and are ready to enter into an agreement.

One issue the parties should consider is whether to limit the agreement to the specific conflict or to look at their interaction or coexistence in a wider perspective. The point is that while the conflict may have been resolved, the atmosphere between the parties may still provide a breeding ground for conflicts, and the agreement phase might offer an opportunity for constructive relationship building.

Therefore, ask the parties if they are interested in looking at their relationship as a whole, considering possible improvements. This could be about exploring old connectors and also new ones (see p. 151). For instance, a solution on joint use of land may be accompanied by agreements on trade, communications, joint access to facilities in the area and cooperation on sports or cultural arrangements.

If the parties are positive, this may be a pleasant phase of the negotiations, not about disagreements but about mutually rewarding possibilities.

Drawing up an agreement

An agreement is to be established, written down and read out to the parties. Be specific:

- What is to happen?
- Who is to do what? When?
- What shall each party do to ensure implementation?
- How will they avoid similar problems in the future?

The need for practical follow-up should be thoroughly assessed and spelled out clearly in the agreement. Be meticulous about formulation to avoid confusion or disagreement later on. Follow-up meetings, possibly with the mediator's participation, are often required. Fix a time for such meetings. We often see parties fail at this point, considering the problem solved after making an agreement. Some international agreements, including the Oslo Agreement, have been criticised on such grounds.

A timeline for specific arrangements may be needed. To ensure that the parties stay aware of their relationship, arrangements that are not meant to last should not be allowed to fizzle out and cause uncertainty. They should either come to an agreed end or be replaced by a renewed agreement.

You may also need to suggest that the parties agree on a mechanism for resolution of possible conflicts in the future.

What if you are asked to contribute to a solution?

Can you, for instance, provide flour or grain to a party in a land conflict till they can cultivate alternative land? One concern is that such contributions may create dependency and could possibly be exploited by the parties in the future. But even if you think a contribution from your organisation is feasible and appropriate, you should think twice before proposing it. Are you absolutely sure that you can live up to the expectations? (Also remember the problem with promises, outlined on p. 91.) Are you confident that you are not jeopardising your impartiality or neutrality? It is generally advisable to avoid a situation where contributions from your organisation are a precondition for the parties' agreement.

Signing the minutes

The parties should ideally sign the minutes and/or the agreement at the end of the meeting and receive a copy at once. It may, however, be necessary to write the documents later, in which case you may send them to the parties or bring them for signature to the next meeting.

The language of the agreement must be comprehensible to all involved, including the mediator and her superiors. This often means that the agreement will have to be written in your working language as well the local language. The agreement must state which version prevails.

If no agreement is reached

If the negotiations are unsuccessful, try to reach an agreement on how to handle the disagreement. One approach is to note points of interest with a view to a later meeting, which must be fixed. If so, ask both the parties to continue working on the issues that are to be dealt with.

What do you do in case of deadlock?

Should the matter be put on ice? Can escalation be avoided? Should there be a separate agreement on this? How can the parties live with the conflict with the least possible problems? Are there problems or challenges outside the conflict that the parties can cooperate on? The parties should try to agree on as much as possible. Remember that conflicts sometimes change rapidly. It may be wise to agree to meet for a review after a specified time even if the chances look meagre.

Follow up on agreements

Agreements may be fragile

Implementation may be frustrated by the influence of other people, by practical problems, by expense, etc. The good atmosphere that led to the agreement may be dispelled after a while, particularly if the problems that led to the conflict recur. Everything agreed upon must of course be implemented. In addition, possible means of support for the agreement should be considered.

Support efforts outside the conflict

Help the parties assess whether they can support the agreement through positive interaction in other contexts. This could include the elements mentioned on p. 53 under 'Expanded scope', but any practical effort that implies positive interaction between the parties may enhance the chances that the agreement will hold.[13]

Such possibilities may also emerge over time. Active follow-up should therefore be a continuous process. Remember that even if an agreement is breached, any positive interaction between the parties may have a dampening effect on the conflict.

Observation and follow-up meetings

Several meetings should generally be arranged to follow up on implementation. If you have agreed to chair them, you could ask the parties to observe what works well between the meetings and what they find positive or acceptable in their interaction. The purpose here is to develop a positive focus.

The brief therapy approach

Brief therapy psychologists handling family conflicts might start their mediation by asking the parties to rate their relationship on a scale from 0 to 10. When they meet again after a week or two, they are asked to reassess the relationship. In a situation where the parties wish to improve the relationship, they are more inclined to see positive aspects and to rate it higher. If so, this will be an experience of positive change and contribute to a positive focus.

This method may in principle be used in any kind of conflict. If you decide to use it, remember to emphasise any improvement in their ratings to the parties. Ask them to explain in each other's presence what has improved. This will reinforce the positive focus and facilitate follow-up. If the rating does not improve, there may be a need to change direction.

Another possibility may be to agree that the parties should inform each other whenever they see an improvement or sign of progress.

Must you follow up?

We have observed that possible support from your organisation should not be a precondition for an agreement between the parties. Still, there may be situations where you find it appropriate to support the implementation. Coverage of humanitarian needs may be essential. If your organisation decides to contribute practically, you may wish to develop your own follow-up scheme. Note specifically what you are to do when. If new possibilities emerge in the course of time, consider including them in your plans. The more attentively you can follow the implementation, the better your chances of making a positive contribution.

One kind of follow-up you should never overlook is praise for the parties' efforts and positive feedback, not only on achievements but on any attempt at positive change.

Rules of thumb for the process of mediation

Procedure

- Learn as much as possible about the conflict and the parties.
- Help them prepare for the process.
- Help them define the overriding goals of the process.
- Get their explicit consent to 'traffic rules', including mutual respect.
- Help them make a strategy if needed.
- Help them assess possible shortcuts to a solution.
- Help them clarify their positions and avoid misunderstandings.

- Help them identify underlying interests together.
- Help them identify all possibilities of meeting those interests.
- Help them identify realistic solutions/steps towards positive change.
- Assist them in developing a clear agreement, possibly an expanded one.
- Make them agree on practical follow-up and if needed a conflict resolution mechanism.

Principles

- Help the parties assume a positive focus.
- Invite them to take responsibility for the process.
- Be on the lookout for all good possibilities, including any outside the conflict. Follow them up.
- Pin down the parties' positive reactions, attitudes and thoughts. Make them visible. Explicitly observe all progress.
- Focus on mutual interests.
- Crack down on interruptions and breaches of other traffic rules.

Notes

1 According to TV reports on the Geneva negotiations on Syria in January 2014, evacuation of civilians from Homs was a topic addressed before the more fundamental conflict issues.
2 For a discussion of this point see Moore (2003).
3 For a thorough discussion of the pre-mediation process, see Galtung (1998).
4 How difficult this can be was demonstrated in TV coverage on 21 January 2014 of the Geneva negotiations between the Syrian government and opposition groups, who disregarded Secretary-General Ban Ki-moon's request to refrain from accusations in their opening statements.
5 For elaboration on the issue in a therapy context, see de Shazer (1988).
6 For details of this approach, see Albrecht and Albrecht (1993).
7 Albrecht and Albrecht (1993) suggest joint identification of a number of balanced optional packages. The parties would then agree on one package and refine it together.
8 Some international agreements defer contentious issues to a later stage, apparently in order to avoid a collapse of the negotiations. The lack of clarity on the right to oil resources between Sudan and South Sudan appears to be an example.
9 In some cases a partial agreement may be of particular value. If so, it may be worth using the opportunity when it appears.
10 For details see Fisher and Ury (1991).
11 Arbitration means that the parties authorise a third party to make a binding decision.
12 Successful mediation will normally imply some elements of reconciliation.
13 We must, however, always observe the special concerns related to cooperation between adversaries (see p. 128).

References

Albrecht, K. and Albrecht, S. (1993) *Added Value Negotiating. The Breakthrough Method for Building Balanced Deals*, Homewood, IL: Business One Irwin.

de Shazer, S. (1988) *Clues. Investigating Solutions in Brief Therapy*, New York: W. W. Norton.
Fischer, R. and Ury, W. (1991) *Getting to yes*, New York: Penguin Books.
Galtung, J. (1998) *Peace by Peaceful Means,* Delhi: Sage Publications.
Moore, C. W. (2003) *The Mediation Process*, San Francisco; Jossey Bass.
Pruitt, D. G. and Rubin, J. Z. (1986) *Social Conflict, Escalation and Settlement*, 3rd edition, New York: McGraw-Hill.

5 Influence

Psychology versus traditional approaches

After the war in Bosnia ended in 1995, a considerable number of international forces and organisations were deployed to ensure peace and implementation of the Dayton Agreement. An area named Velika Kladusa/Cazin in the north-west of Bosnia faced a particular challenge. The Bosnian politician Ficret Abdic had during the war twice seized power in a local 'war within the war', once with the support of Bosnia's Serbian enemies. When the war ended and Abdic had been thrown out, more than 20,000 people from this area were living in exile in Croatia. Most of them were regarded as Abdic supporters and thus traitors. On returning home they faced a tough reception, not only from civilians belonging to the other political side, but also from local police and military forces. Men suspected of having served Abdic were apprehended for interrogation and often abused. The protection unit of UNHCR was among the organisations engaged in ensuring the safe return of refugees. At first its approach was to avoid informing the local police of the returns. After some time the strategy was changed and if they tried instead, partly in cooperation with other organisations, to bring about a change in the police's attitude and behaviour.

After a few months the situation had changed. The protection officers would now bring lists of names and addresses of returning refugees to the local police commander, and request him to send patrols to the returnees' villages to protect them against other civilians. This was done. The number of reports of abuse dropped significantly, and in general the level of security in the area was substantially improved.

How did this change take place? What techniques are available in such situations? We are going to look at some relevant approaches, and shall come back to the example of Velika Kladusa later in the chapter.

When mediation is impossible

International delegates often find that parties to a conflict cannot meet to negotiate, typically when a strong party suppresses a weak one (for example, soldiers vs civilian minority or guard vs prisoners). The same is the case where equal parties are so strongly opposed to each other that normal communication is impossible.

It may be your mandate to try to do something about such situations. Various approaches are possible. Depending on the situation, you may report to superiors, authorities or international bodies. You may also intervene via persons or groups that can exert influence. This may, however, be time-consuming, and the time aspect may be critical. The result is also often uncertain.

In many cases, your only possibility of achieving anything will be to try to intervene directly vis-à-vis one party or the parties separately. This may happen in different ways. You may try to influence the parties' perception of each other, but that is often a heavy task. Another angle is to train the parties separately in conflict management, and, through the training, help them understand each other's situation. This will take time, however, and if the conflict is strong and the power unbalanced, the stronger party will probably reject such an approach. We shall therefore look at a model of change based on more direct approaches.

Influence on behaviour and attitudes

How can you make a party to a conflict change behaviour? Human beings are all the time exposed to influences of various kinds, sometimes leading to changes in behaviour and attitude. Knowledge of how people influence each other's behaviour is a powerful tool in a conflict context.

Let us look at some aspects of influence and techniques you may use in your work.

We are not going to discriminate between influences on attitude and on behaviour. The relevant techniques may be termed as attitude change through change of behaviour. As shown below, changed behaviour also influences attitude. Assuming that you aim at long-term goals in your work, attitude change is often a necessity.

Roles, norms and expectations

A social role may be defined as a set of expectations attached to a position or function in society.

A norm may be defined as the expectations that arise every time a social situation occurs. We face norms and role expectations everywhere, and our behaviour is closely connected to them. Expectations come from the environment we live in. Partly subconsciously, we also expect ourselves to live up to different roles and norms. A humanitarian delegate is expected to help people in need. A soldier is expected to fight under certain circumstances. You perform a number of roles in your daily life, as son or daughter, father or mother, spouse, colleague, friend, etc. And you constantly face social situations where norms influence what you do, for example when you act as a driver, pedestrian, participant in a course, etc.

The power of the role

The social psychologist Philip Zimbardo did an experiment in 1973 that dramatically illustrates the power of the role. Arranging a mock prison in the basement of Stanford University, he and his team engaged 12 students to play the roles of guards and prisoners. The roles were distributed by throwing dice. The guards were equipped with khaki uniforms, whistles, batons and reflecting sunglasses, whereas the prisoners got loose-fitting smocks, sandals and a chain attached to one leg.

The idea was to monitor the group for two weeks, to observe whether they lived up to their roles. After six days the experiment had to be terminated. The guards developed oppressive behaviour and showed creativity in tormenting and humiliating the prisoners, who, for their part, became passive, helpless and withdrawn. Some of the prisoners became so timid and depressed that they had to leave the experiment even earlier (Zimbardo and Leippe, 1991).

When behaviour can be influenced like this in a situation we know is a game, one can easily imagine how influential real roles are. Therefore, roles and expectations hold a key to change.

War is a striking example of what real roles can make us do. Young men, who in peacetime have civilian professions, are expected to leave them and assume roles as soldiers, expected to fight. In extreme cases, they may be expected to commit cruel acts, as seen in cases of ethnic cleansing. Then the war comes to an end, and the young men are expected to go back to their civilian professions, where once again peaceful work is expected. There may also be elements of force, authority and other influence behind such changes, but role expectations clearly play an important part.

From a negative to a positive role

When intervening with one party in a conflict, you may often face the challenge of moving a person from a negative to a positive role; in other words, have him assume a peaceful role instead of an aggressive one. Let us assume that it is your task to get a police commander to abandon his role as an abuser and adopt another one, for instance as a protector of a vulnerable group. Influencing a change of roles may happen in different ways, but here we assume that you try to exert direct personal influence, and that you have access to communication with the police commander.

The task may be simpler than you think. Given that you are seeking to bring about indisputably positive changes, you have access to a powerful weapon. People have a general need to feel good about themselves. We wish to see ourselves as sensible, reasonable and just, and we want others to see us the same way. Even what total strangers think of us means something. In a first meeting, most of us try to make a good impression. This feels even more important in relations with someone we respect or who commands authority. The same pertains if a friendly tone or an element of sympathy is established.

Statements – a basis for change!

If you ask an 'evil police commander' how he relates to a victimised group, he will normally depict a positive role for himself. A typical statement would be that he is concerned with everybody's security and that he tries to protect the victimised group as well as others. This is an opportunity served on a silver tray. What the police commander does is to place himself in a positive role vis-à-vis you. If you can help him establish himself in this role, you have ensured a basis for change. How do you do it?

Supporting good statements: the martial arts effect

An effective way is to express support. Let us assume that the police commander has depicted a positive picture of himself and his attitudes. Your response might be: 'I am very happy to hear about your view. Our organisation has exactly the same concerns. We wish to support measures that may improve security for the vulnerable group and we are very interested in discussing cooperation with you.'

What you do here, to borrow a term from martial arts, is to utilise your opponent's momentum. You strike at the right moment and support him when he makes a statement in the direction you want, moving from a negative to a positive role. You might even express joy at his position if it feels natural. By giving active support to what he says, you achieve the following:

- You confirm the role expectations that he has induced himself.
- You help him to move in the direction you wish.
- You allow him to create an element of positive commitment vis-à-vis you.
- You let him initiate psychological mechanisms for positive change that will be described later.

Role reinforcement

Once your counterpart has adopted a positive approach towards an issue, the next step will be to confirm and reinforce this role. In addition to expressing support, the following steps are recommended:

1 *Make him repeat or confirm the statement, and if possible elaborate on it.* This should happen immediately, but use later occasions too. Give a positive response to every positive statement.
2 *Expect other positive statements*. Pose questions on related issues that may reinforce the positive stand he has taken. Each positive statement you achieve may become a contribution to his new role. Let him reinforce the picture of himself as a good and respectable person. Much will follow as logical consequences. 'Once you have said A …'
3 *It is important to pin down statements on values that he stands for himself.* These feel obliging and as we shall see, such statements may have a strong

influence. But don't advance too fast. If you expect too much too soon, he may counter-react. Small steps are important.

4 *Spread expectations of positive developments to others*, for instance by informing opinion leaders, other organisations, involved groups or media. Remember that he is probably facing negative expectations from other environments, and the idea is to build up the heaviest possible counterbalance to this.
5 *Tell him about the positive expectations being spread.* 'I am glad to brief my headquarters or government, the press, other international organisations, peacekeeping forces about your positive attitude.' As he becomes aware of these positive expectations, his perception will be reinforced, and so will his feeling of commitment.
6 Try to have others contact him with expectations of positive acts, so that he experiences their expectations in practice.
7 *Establish contexts where he cannot go back on a commitment.* One example is to invite him to meetings with important persons or groups where his positive statements are made known and may be followed up by others. These efforts will jointly enforce positive expectations. They will come from:
   - you
   - others involved or being informed
   - himself, because of his commitment.

Consistency: why statements commit

Because of our need to feel good about ourselves, we need to feel rational and reliable, and we need others to see us that way. No one wishes to be seen as inclined to change their opinion without good reason. If we have evoked certain expectations, we will in general feel committed to them. The clearer and more public our statements, the more committed we feel.

During the Korean war the Chinese army imprisoned a number of American soldiers. The Chinese wanted the prisoners to embrace communist ideology and make pro-China statements that could be used in propaganda. The process would begin by having the soldiers (without force) make seemingly totally innocent statements. One question might be 'Is everything good in the US?' and the answer would perhaps be, 'No, everything is not good in the US'. Next the soldier might be asked to give examples of what was not good in the US. Having specified verbally what was not good, he would be requested to write a list and sign it. Later, in a discussion meeting, he might be asked to read aloud what he had written. The next step could be to ask the soldier to write an article on the subject. With very small steps the soldiers were moved in the desired direction.

Later the article and the name of the soldier could be used publicly in radio broadcasts. These would reach other prison camps and the American forces. The soldier would now feel trapped in a collaborator role, and this would be used to extract even more pro-communist statements from him. Other soldiers would see him as inclined towards communism, something that would unavoidably

Table 5.1 Positive and negative statements

Positive statements	*Negative statements*
I wish to protect all.	Group X has inflicted problems on itself.
I can understand how group X has become like that.	Group X was after us.
Group Y has tried to bring about a peaceful development.	It is impossible to communicate with people from group X.
It is possible to solve the conflict.	Group X is criminal.

influence his self-image in the same direction. Many soldiers came back to the US after the war with political ideas that were considerably changed (Cialdini, 1993).

Problems in obtaining positive statements

Let us go back to the 'evil' police commander. You may find it strange to hunt for positive statements. One suggestion is to pose questions pertaining specifically to the moral attitude of your counterpart. Here you will normally get positive statements, which are likely to induce a feeling of personal commitment. But even without such questions our police commander will normally come up with statements that may be used. Let us try to illustrate this. We imagine a conversation with the commander, who belongs to group Y, which persecutes and abuses members of group X. We imagine that the local police do not give any protection to group X, and to some extent commit abuses themselves. In a conversation with the commander, some of what he says will normally go in a positive direction, and some in a negative direction.

The statements in the left-hand column in Table 5.1 may all be utilised to establish a positive role. Pin them down. Ask for elaboration and confirm that you agree.

The hunt for positive signals

What if, after all, you don't manage to get any positive statements? Sometimes a more conscious search for positive signals is required. Such signals may be found in both statements and body language. Let us take a look at how the experienced negotiator, for example in the sales sector, performs.

Like a silent witness, she watches her counterpart in the conversation. In these circumstances, even the most reserved speaker will reveal different reactions and attitudes, some in a negative, others in a positive, direction, depending on what we are after. Positive signals may be a nod, a smile, a positive facial expression or some other kind of body language. At the slightest positive signal the witness will strike, asking her counterpart a question on the issue that seemed to arouse his positive response. As soon she gets a positive statement, she will follow up by stating facts or concretising the issue, repeating and confirming possible agreement, perhaps also appreciating or expressing joy at the counterpart's attitude. The witness will consecutively support all her counterpart's 'good' statements. At the end, when the counterpart is sufficiently firm in his position, the time has come to suggest action based on the position expressed.

Used with caution, this technique may be extremely effective. Just as the skilled marketing professional uses the method in sales contexts, you may use it in the cause of peace.

Time for action!

This is an important step. We now have the good positions of the 'evil' police commander out in the open, and we have pinned them down and confirmed them to the best of our ability. It is time for him to bear the consequences. Tell him, for example, that you need his help in a concrete matter. This might be to send a patrol to a village where abuse has been reported or to look into a complaint about police violence. It is important to start modestly. Choose questions where you are quite certain you will get a yes.

Once you have got a yes, show appreciation, and agree on how to proceed together, for example by meeting again next week. This is only supposed to be the beginning. You are to bring about a series of actions in the same direction. Remember, for each positive act he performs, his feeling of being committed to the good cause is being reinforced.

Positive response to positive action

Any positive action should be followed by a positive response. Be meticulous about this. Little is more inspiring than recognition, and little is more demotivating than good efforts passing unnoticed.[1] The effects of a positive response are:

- He feels appreciated and thus comfortable in the role.
- It becomes attractive to make further efforts.
- His commitment is strengthened.

Make sure that all who might exert a positive influence get to know about his efforts, and if possible have them contribute with their own positive response. It is particularly effective if you can prompt such a response from his 'enemies' or victims. The moment an abuser notices that the oppressed have started expecting positive action from his side, for example protection, then an important development may have started.

Practical cooperation for a good cause

Try to establish positive cooperation to the greatest extent possible. You may, for example, agree to meet regularly to discuss challenges or reports. Bringing the police commander along to meet victims or do a site assessment is recommended, but not until he is ready for it. The victims must also accept it.

Any form of positive cooperation will strengthen his feeling of positive expectations and thus reinforce his commitment and motivation. Additionally, the cooperation will give you the possibility of following up with reinforcement and further development of the role expectations. The cooperation may also evoke sympathy, and hence a wish for continued cooperation.

Remember, the good role is attractive. We have established how important our need for a positive self-image is. When helping a police commander into a positive role, you offer him such a self-image. Most of us are probably not very happy about abusing our enemies. There is reason to believe that we are happier with a self-image where we stand for ethical values. We get these values confirmed through recognition from others. This may, of course, clash with the expectations of some, but the good deed may in itself satisfy the needs of the individual.

An Indian study from 1996 on corruption at the work place showed that those who considered corruption a necessity for success, were highly unsatisfied with their work situation (Viswesvaran and Deshpande, 1996).

Cognitive dissonance: clash between act and attitude

Cognitive refers to psychological process related to thinking, understanding, formation of beliefs, attitudes and more The term 'cognitive dissonance' is used when we experience a conflict between our behaviour and our attitudes. We need to resolve this dissonance. An example: a militia leader has orchestrated terrorist attacks on a group of people. When you come to meet him, he chooses to lie to you, saying he believes in basic human rights for everybody, maybe that he even treats the vulnerable group well. A dissonance now arises between what he says and his real attitude. What happens as a result of such dissonance is that we feel a psychic discomfort that we want to be rid of. Your challenge will be to help the militia leader to get out on the right side.

The power of action

The militia leader's statement has already had a positive influence on him. (A statement is also an act.) Our need to be consistent makes us inclined to adapt to what we have said and done. If we have made positive statements about those we don't like or done something nice to them, we will generally adapt by liking them better afterwards. Simply put, acts defeat thought.

Any positive statement from the militia leader therefore implies a small step of self-influence. After having given a positive statement about his relationship with the vulnerable group, he is likely to hate them slightly less, and it becomes a little less attractive to continue the terror. This effect is reinforced with each positive statement you get from him.

Let us assume that you manage further to have the militia leader follow up his statement with practical action, for example by agreeing to protect some vulnerable individuals or group. The change in attitude will now be reinforced. When doing something positive for others, our need for consistency makes us think more positively of them afterwards.

This influence is reinforced through every positive act, which in its turn makes it more natural to do another. What we effectively get is a spiral towards positive development. If this continues unbroken, the militia leader will, in the end, have a positive attitude towards the said persons and the dissonance will be gone.

NB The more clearly a position is expressed, and the more relevance it has for a person's ethical values, the stronger the dissonance effect will be.

The Benjamin Franklin effect

Cognitive dissonance may also be used to influence a person who has a negative attitude towards you.

Benjamin Franklin (1706–1790), known not only for the lightning conductor but also for a marvellous political career and a rare ability to influence others, learned how to use this kind of influence consciously, long before science identified the phenomenon.

Attempting to influence a politician who had taken a hostile stand towards him, Franklin one day asked him if he could borrow a certain book from him. The response was a reluctant yes and they agreed that the book would be returned after one week. Franklin returned the book on time. Extending hearty thanks, he emphasised that the book had been very useful to him. From that day, the opponent was more positive towards him, and they came to enjoy a lasting friendship (Aronson *et al.*, 1999).

Try the technique yourself!

Among your acquaintances or colleagues there is surely someone you don't like very much. Try to do this person a favour or some kindness. Alternatively, defend him or her next time he or she is being criticised. Observe how you think and feel about this person afterwards.

The danger of negative acts

It is important to remember that doing something negative to a person has the opposite effect. Soldiers abusing defenceless civilians tend to reduce the feeling of dissonance by hating their victims and derogating them. If, despite your efforts, negative influence makes the militia leader continue the terror, you will not succeed.

To ensure a positive outcome, try to put a halt to the negative action over a period of time. For example, actively follow up the positive expectations he has evoked through his statements. You may then have a period where positive action and thus positive influence prevail, and positive change happens. The recipe, once dissonance is established in the mind of your 'evil' counterpart, is as follows:

- Support the positive position.
- Help her reinforce it.
- Try to bring about positive acts based on the position.
- Try to bring the negative action to a halt for a period of time.
- Use appreciation to make her aware of her positive action.

You will recognise the procedure from the section on roles, norms and expectations (p. 60). The point is that the technique suggested to induce a change of role is also effective because of cognitive dissonance.

Exceptions to the dissonance effect

There are two aspects you should bear in mind.

White lies

A person lying or playing a role for strong external reasons may avoid the feeling of dissonance. If the said militia leader wants to protect his group against punishment, he may deny perpetrating abuses. If so, he may see the lie as necessary and justified and thus avoid feeling much dissonance.

As previously observed, it is wise to ask for his personal view on ethical topics where he does not need to lie to save anybody. In that case the lie will give him an integrity problem. His desire to give a positive picture of himself is not enough to avoid dissonance. Thus he cannot avoid being influenced.

Poor self-image

A person who is convinced that he is unreliable or prone to bluffing may not feel dissonance when he is lying. Such persons are, however, rare.

Very few of us can escape the influence of cognitive dissonance, and it is well worth trying out when you need to exert influence in a conflict.

Role-play

It might happen that the evil militia leader or police commander plays some kind of a game vis-à-vis you, and that in his heart he thinks, 'To hell with minority X', while at the same time cooperating with you in protecting them. Does this mean he is not being influenced?

Psychological research has shown that even downright lies influence us. Additionally, from the example with guards and prisoners we know that we are easily influenced by our roles, and that we inevitably experience a degree of identification. Role-plays are therefore an effective way of influencing attitudes. Should you perform a role as a militia leader in a war situation, you will be more understanding of his attitudes than you were before.

Even if you know that a militia leader or police commander is playing the role of nice guy with you, you should still act as if his role is real. This will increase the effect. He will, through the performance, exert a positive influence on himself. And on your side, you can use your imagination to follow up with everything you know about role reinforcement. This will increase the chances that he stays in the role and develops it.

You may in general grasp and utilise any 'role-play' that you find in conflict contexts. Helping a person change from a negative to a positive role is sometimes astonishingly easy.

A UN refugee camp in Africa was being plagued by theft, and the camp manager wanted to do something about it. She considered it obvious that the culprits were a gang of unemployed young men who used to hang around the camp like vultures. She took a chance and employed the whole gang as guards. She told them about the problems the thefts were causing to the humanitarian work, and said that she depended totally on their help to solve the problem. They received a decent salary and food for their work. She followed up with praise and acknowledgement, and she demanded respect for them among the camp's residents. The arrangement worked perfectly. The incidence of theft dropped to almost zero, and the humanitarian work became easier.

To begin with, working as guards was probably some kind of role-play to the gang, but it apparently had a positive influence from the very beginning. She reinforced the influence the best she could, and the actors found their roles attractive. After a while she considered them really reliable guards. In addition to the effect of the role-play itself, a number of the young men's basic needs were fulfilled. They achieved respect, recognition, physical need fulfilment, perhaps also a feeling of meaning in their lives through useful work and positive feedback. You may appreciate that some of the same fulfilment was offered to the 'evil' police commander who got the opportunity to play a positive role.

In international contexts, we have seen striking changes of role and behaviour. Many considered Yasser Arafat a terrorist in his early career, but he later assumed the role of a statesman. Gandhi moved from the role of a lawyer to become a spiritual leader. Imagine that you intervene in a conflict between two parties, and that you manage to get both of them into a role where they perceive themselves as skilled conflict managers, who see positive transformation as their responsibility. The possibilities are in principle unlimited. If you can get key persons to play positive roles, this may have a decisive impact on the development of a conflict.

The yes technique and the danger of no

The yes technique

If we need acceptance or a positive response from a counterpart, one method is what we may call the 'yes technique'. This method, often used in sales contexts, is based on the use of so-called yes questions, meaning questions to which you count on a positive response.

A clever salesman may use a strategy based on a series of questions where the likely answer is yes. Starting very cautiously, he would pose a question to which yes is the obvious answer. He would then take one small step further with another question where yes is ensured. In this way he will continue with new questions, each building on the previous one, till he addresses the questions that really matter. The essence of the technique is that it brings us into a yes attitude.

As we have observed, our need to be consistent means that we are being influenced by what we do. Through a series of yes responses we assume a positive attitude, and will be inclined to continue answering yes. And every little yes paves the way for acceptance of the next question. (Remember the technique of the Chinese during the Korean war, p. 63.)

Those who really use the technique effectively pin down every single yes with a positive response, appreciation or maybe even gratitude. This is combined with repetition and confirmation of each point, all to make the counterpart feel committed.

The danger of no

In the same way as every yes can bring you closer to your objective, each no may take you further away. This may lead to a no attitude, and the one who says no to an important question from you may assume an attitude of reluctance. Remember, we like people less after having done something negative to them. Therefore, if you have to ask for something important, first try to move into a position where a yes is likely. If this is not possible, try to use words that keep your counterpart in a role where she is expected to help you. For example, 'Do you think it is possible for you to help me with this?' The question assumes that she wishes to help you, even if she is unable to. This reduces the danger of her no changing her positive attitude towards you.

'From more to less'

It may still happen that you expect a no but have to ask for something. Let us assume that you are trying to save an exposed group from an expected assault, and need assistance from an uncooperative military leader. One technique often used in marketing and fundraising is called 'from more to less'.[2] The approach is to start by asking for more than you really want by forwarding a request that is likely to be turned down. Upon rejection you go directly to wish number two which is far more modest.

Imagine that you need support to evacuate 50 people. If you start by asking the military leader if he can evacuate 150 people and provide food and accommodation for them for three months, it may be obvious that he will say no. But the question may increase the chances that he afterwards agrees to evacuate 50. The theory behind the technique is that we seem to give something by reducing or abandoning our first request, and that this concession on our part should solicit a concession from our counterpart. In addition, a request seems more modest if it follows a more comprehensive one.

The technique must be used with great caution, if at all. If the first request is totally unrealistic, request number two will probably not be met either. In that case, the reduction will not be seen as real and you might also risk losing face.

On good communication

Good communication is important in all forms of conflict management, but several issues dealt with in this section are of particular importance in an influence context.

We have earlier underscored that when communicating, content as well as form must comply with the recipient's need for a positive self-image. If your counterpart in a discussion feels that this need is being fulfilled, he is likely to feel comfortable and be more open and positive, and the chances of positive interaction increase.

Empathy and active listening

A precondition for positive interaction is normally that you understand your counterpart's positions and the thinking behind them. Empathy may simply be defined as the ability to identify with others and understand what they feel and stand for. It sounds obvious that empathy implies active and focused listening, but the fact is that active listening does not come for free. It demands consciousness and practice. Many eminent negotiators have made it a daily habit to practise active listening. Listening, of course, implies that we focus on what others say, identify what is important and concentrate on understanding and remembering it. But what does active listening mean?

Through listening you prepare to answer, comment on, and otherwise relate to what is being said. This requires activity. It may be necessary to take notes, pose questions, and possibly sum up your counterpart's positions after his presentation. (If you want to take notes, make sure this is acceptable, and that your counterpart does not fear that her statements will be reported.) Use a high degree of eye contact, and let your body language show your positive interest.

Paraphrasing

This is an element in active listening, also called the mirror technique. It basically means repeating a counterpart's statements in one's own words. The technique is used to address facts, as well as the emotions and needs behind a statement. The purpose of paraphrasing is to:

- help you understand your counterpart;
- make your counterpart feel understood;
- defuse strong emotions (to this end rewording of harsh statements may be needed);
- offer both parties time to reflect on what is being said;
- clarify the subject.

Let us take a meeting where a mayor lashes out at you because he thinks your organisation has written biased reports on incidents of violence, blaming his supporters. A good reply may be: 'Am I correct to observe that you think we have wrongly blamed your supporters for the incident?' And if the answer is yes, I understand that you are angry because of this, and need to know that our reports are correct.'

A series of paraphrasing questions may sometimes have a very positive impact on the atmosphere. An angry Palestinian participant in a seminar on communication once shouted 'murderer!' to the convenor, Marshall Rosenberg. The reason was that he was opposed to US provision of military equipment to Israel. After questioning the man for 10 minutes, using the paraphrasing technique to address his thoughts and feelings, Rosenberg finally explained his own view to the man, who afterwards invited him home for dinner (Rosenberg, 1999).

You will have to feel your way as to what extent your counterpart is susceptible to paraphrasing. Some may act negatively to a series of paraphrasing questions, but more often you may find that people appreciate them as expressions of empathy and respect. Try it out in private contexts.

During the listening process you also have the possibility of exerting discreet influence. We have earlier described positive responses to positive statements in order to help a person into a positive role. You may also give such a response through your body language. When your counterpart gives a positive statement, you may express approval or support through nods, smiles, eye contact, hand movements, etc.

Examples of active listening

The following examples are largely borrowed from Woodhouse and Duffey (2009).

ENCOURAGING

'Tell us some more'; 'Could you explain what happened?'

ACKNOWLEDGING

Verbal: 'I believe I understand'; 'I see'; 'That sounds important to you.' Non-verbal: nodding, eye contact, hand gestures, open body language.

CHECKING

'Am I right in thinking you said ...?'; 'I understand you are angry about this.'

CLARIFYING

'I am not sure I understand'; 'Did you say ...?'

EMPATHY

'I believe I understand why you are worried by this'; 'I think this situation has been very difficult for you.'

REFLECTING

'You are upset? What particularly is upsetting you?'

SUMMARISING

'There seems to be several important issues here.'

Sensitivity to counter-arguments

Counter-arguments are a natural part of discussions. Most of us, however, are not very receptive to them. We are inclined to perceive counter-arguments as suggestions that we are wrong, and it is never nice to admit being wrong. It is therefore tempting to close one's ears to a counterpart's arguments and focus on one's own instead. A good negotiator is open to counter-arguments. Often other people are simply right, but even if they are wrong they have to be taken seriously. Even when a counterpart stands for something you condemn morally, it is important to be open. In the arguments beneath the immoral position there may be sensible or logical points of view, and as a rule you should give a positive response to these. The reasons beneath the immoral position may offer a starting point for discussion. There may also be emotions that need to be aired. If your counterpart feels respected, you open up positive communication even if disagreeing with his positions.

Respect

Our need for respect is extremely important. This is closely connected to our need for a positive self-image. However much you need respect as a representative of an international organisation, it is important for everyone you interact with to feel respected. The feeling of being respected makes it easier to relax, to open up to the views of others and to communicate constructively. On the other hand, a person who does not feel respected will react negatively towards her counterparts, making positive interaction difficult. When we intervene to address the needs of others, respect is high among the values we are supposed to promote; this should be a rule of conduct. Sadly, it is sometimes forgotten.

After the war in north-west Bosnia, local authorities complained occasionally about international military personnel behaving arrogantly. The complaints included reckless driving of tanks, humiliation of local police, etc. This changed with improved contact between the forces and the local police, after regular meetings had been established between representatives of the UN forces, the UN police and local police leaders.

Understanding

Benjamin Franklin (p. 67) habitually made a point of stating that he understood his counterpart. His view was that it is nearly always possible to understand your counterpart's position or how he reached it, even if his points of view are very unreasonable. Understanding may in fact be a magic formula. This, too, is connected to our need for a positive self-image. What you normally achieve by expressing understanding is that your counterpart leans back thinking, 'Ah, this person understands me! This is one human being I can communicate with.'

Once you have achieved this reaction, you may often express strong disagreement and still communicate well. If articulating the same disagreement without expressing understanding, you have a much more uphill process. And if you state bluntly that you don't understand your counterpart's position, you are likely to face resentment and defensive attitudes, even if you don't differ much in positions. Try the alternatives yourself in private discussions.

In other words, express understanding as far as you can. If you understand either the words or the thinking behind them, you will be in a position to say: 'I understand what you are saying' or 'I understand how you think'. That you yourself have a different standpoint is a different matter.

Sometimes tense people may reject expressions of understanding, contending that 'You cannot possibly understand me!' If you sense that your counterpart is very tense or emotional, you may choose the wording: 'I believe I understand you' or 'Please let me see if I understand you correctly', and then try some simple paraphrasing.

Agreeing

We have underscored the significance of agreeing in several contexts. What is it that makes it important? Expressing agreement is a strong kind of support that may meet your counterpart's need for respect, understanding and appreciation, and can thus be a solid contribution to his self-respect. What you offer when expressing agreement is, in other words, important need fulfilment. Agreement may in addition:

- establish a basis for sympathy;
- be a positive experience one may like to repeat;

- establish similarity (p. 79) and so pave the way for influence;
- serve as a basis for agreement;
- support positive role development.

This is why negotiations should include establishing points of agreement early on. In an influence perspective it is recommended to utilise all the agreement that can be found.

Even in conversations between enemies there would normally be statements on which both parties agree. This may be utilised. Whether in mediation or in intervention vis-à-vis one party, emphasise all agreement as clearly as possible, verbally or through distinctive body language such as facial expressions, nods and hand movements. Use direct eye contact to emphasise agreement. State as clearly as possible what you agree on. You might express joy or even gratitude, if natural.

Can practical consequences be drawn from the agreement? If so, draw the conclusions jointly. The more agreement, the more commitment. And the more points of agreement you find, the more you facilitate cooperation. As observed in connection with courtesy calls, when a meeting ends, use the moment of farewell for a micro summing up and seal the agreement through a firm handshake, again accompanied by eye contact.

If you wish to test the power of agreement in practice, try this experiment. Next time a counterpart in a discussion makes a statement you disagree with, don't say so. Tell him instead that you agree, but that you have a slightly different angle or some additional points of view. You will most probably find that your counterpart reacts positively to what you say. He may even agree.

Are you worth listening to?

This is about both form and content.

Your presentation

How you use your voice is important. You have to speak audibly, clearly and concisely enough to be heard and understood, but not necessarily loudly all the time. In noisy discussions, skilled negotiators sometimes catch attention by lowering their voice when getting the floor. Try to observe in groups what gains you the most attention. Varying your voice level may also add life to the presentation and underline points, as may a certain voice intensity, provided it sounds natural.

Your eyes are also important. Look at the person you are speaking to. Make sure he/she listens and understands what you say. Some of the best lawyers in court display a very concentrated focus on the judge, watching her actively while presenting their case. In case of any sign of failing attention, they react by raising their voice significantly, seeking eye contact with the judge, who would be hard pushed to escape the message. Looking at someone firmly also serves as confirmation that you stand for what you say.

Body language should be relaxed and positive. Your deportment should also reflect your engagement and interest. The worst you can do is to sit stooping with your arms across your chest and look down at the table. Don't hesitate to use your hands to emphasise a point if it feels natural. This may add life to your presentation.

Are you credible?

We have already touched upon our need to be considered credible and respectable. This is a significant basis for influence. A credible person gives an image of solidity. This induces respect and confidence, attitudes we need to encourage.

Anyone wishing to influence must remember it is important to appear credible. Apart from sticking to your word, this implies never saying more than you can be sure of. If you are in doubt about facts, say so. Be direct and clear on your agency's mandate and its principles. If your assignment includes submitting reports about controversial subjects such as human rights abuse, it may be wise to explain this, as well as the principles the reports are based on.

Authority

We are all influenced by authority. From childhood we have learned to obey authorities of numerous kinds, and we continue to do so throughout life. The more authority you have, the stronger you will be. What gives you authority depends on the context. Relevant factors are:

- title
- who you represent
- how you are dressed
- age
- behaviour, eyes, voice and manners
- comportment and looks
- qualities such as confidence, calm and vigour
- vehicle: type and standard
- education and knowledge.

We observed the importance of establishing authority in connection with courtesy calls (p. 34). This must happen naturally of course, but it may be a good habit to do some mental preparation before important meetings or negotiations. Obviously you have to be well prepared on the subjects of discussion, but if you have a clear picture of yourself in the role you are to fill, you have a better chance of performing with authoritatively.

One piece of advice if your job involves meetings with people much more senior than you: apart from your respective roles, you should consider yourselves equals. A state leader or minister may wish to be addressed as 'Your

Excellency' and it is generally safest to do so unless she suggests otherwise. You must of course also, at all times, be polite. But do not abandon your own confidence. Overly humble persons are rarely interesting counterparts.

Expertise

If you possess some expertise in the field where you are intervening, it may be useful if your counterpart perceives this. Psychological experiments have shown that expertise is a powerful factor of influence, in that experts convince us more easily than others. It may be useful, therefore, if your counterparts get to know of your expertise, but make sure you reveal this in a natural manner. Expertise may refer to your professional speciality such as logistics, communication, engineering, etc. You may also have expertise in more general fields such as international politics or human rights.

Reciprocation

The idea of reciprocation is that we should try to repay in kind what another person has provided to us. This constitutes an important aspect of our lives (see Cialdini, 1993). The idea probably exists in all cultures.

When we do something for people we interact with, a sense of expectation and obligation is created. The reciprocation may take the form of coherent services, in kind, by provisions or in other ways. In marketing and in charity this aspect is utilised skilfully, for example by serving coffee and cakes in stores, or distributing flowers when collecting money for humanitarian purposes.

International delegates operate in many contexts where reciprocation is relevant. In general, one may assume that in any situation where something is rendered beyond what the recipient considers an obligation, reciprocation will be an issue. For example, the aspects described above, like active listening, respect, understanding and agreeing, may be perceived as services rendering it mandatory for your counterpart to give something in return.

When discussing the influence of roles we observed how positive reports and information about the 'evil' police commander may be used to build up positive expectations. The commander himself may come to see your positive reports and similar follow-up as something that must be reciprocated, for example by showing goodwill when you need his cooperation.

This is not to suggest that you should use the reciprocity mechanism uncritically, but you should be aware of it, since the expectation of reciprocation may be a powerful tool of influence. Research indicates that it does not matter much whether or not we like a person who does something for us. We feel obliged to reciprocate.

Bear in mind that obligations go both ways; you must avoid situations where someone expects something from you that you should not render.

Sympathy and friendship

In communication with fellow human beings we are bound to experience both positive and negative feelings. Positive ones may include good chemistry, sympathy, friendship, shared humour, etc. If conscious of them, we can use such feelings constructively.

Sympathy

Sympathy or liking someone is a powerful factor in the psychology of influence. In some ways we are apt to be influenced much more by people we like than by others. We are more inclined to copy or imitate people we like, we agree with them more easily, we accept more from them and are more inclined to do them services. In the field of sales and marketing, this aspect is being consciously exploited. Good salesmen use a host of clever tricks to appear likeable.

What creates sympathy?

You are able to control some of the factors creating sympathy. Clearly, as an international delegate you must relate in a balanced way to parties in conflict. But normally it is possible to make sympathy part of the atmosphere without compromising your balance and integrity. In other words, perform your assignment in such a manner that the parties like you. Even between opponents in war, elements of sympathy may prevail.

General Rommel, known as 'the Desert Fox' even to his opponents in the Second World War, purportedly had difficulties getting along with his Italian allies. The *Encyclopædia Britannica* (1999–2000) states: 'Basically, the British were more to his liking. He was an avid reader of the book of warfare written by Sir Archibald Wavell, the first allied commander in chief in the Middle East and Rommel's opponent in north Africa.'

Typical factors creating sympathy are:

- similarity between the parties
- frequency of encounters
- looks and appearance
- politeness
- respect
- understanding
- agreeing
- contact
- the feeling of being liked
- cooperation.

Most of these elements are described above. Here we shall take a closer look at similarity and frequency of encounters.

Similarity

People similar to each other are more inclined to feel mutual sympathy. This pertains to physical similarity, but also to qualities, attitudes and background. This phenomenon is also frequently utilised in marketing. Don't be surprised if a car salesman discovers that he has relatives in your hometown or finds that you both are interested in outdoor life.

Likewise in international missions, you may find it easier to cooperate if your counterpart has a relative who once lived in your country or if you discover that you share views on questions of importance. (See also 'Agreeing' on pp. 74–75.)

Frequency of encounters

How often we see people influences our sympathy for them. Psychological research in the US has indicated that students attending lectures liked fellow students who attended often better than those who attended rarely, even without interacting with any of them (Aronson *et al.*, 1999). Other research indicates that our choice of friends is closely linked to whom we see often, for example neighbours. If wishing to build a good rapport with someone, this importance of frequent encounters is worth remembering.

The element of friendship

Sympathy often induces an element of friendship. Friendship kindles a wish for positive interaction such as help and services when needed. This means that if you experience a friendly response from an otherwise belligerent militia leader, there might be a possibility of getting his help if you need it. If he does help you, his act will reinforce his friendly attitude towards you. This may also be a step towards a role where he generally does the services you ask of him.

You should of course not get too close to the parties in a conflict. The element of friendship must never collide with your mission and integrity, and you must avoid any dependency impinging on the performance of your duties. In general, you should therefore handle the friendship element with caution. Some may even react negatively to the very thought of friendly relations with a brutal militia leader.

We are, however, only discussing an element of friendship in an otherwise professional context. Socialising is not an issue. Even so, you must consider what kind of interaction you find natural, everything given. Police investigators sometimes make particular use of the friendship element when interrogating accused persons, applying friendship as a tool to reveal the truth, even if the interrogation is part of a criminal prosecution.

An UN police officer posted in north-west Bosnia after the war started spending his time off with local police officers, and vulnerable civilians complained that he used to side with the local police. One night he was attacked by three unknown men and beaten up. He later received anonymous threats of further attacks and left his service.

This example underlines the need to handle the friendship element with delicacy. It is normally possible to have a friendly relationship with both parties in a conflict. The precondition is that you never give the parties reason to doubt your integrity.

The follow-up of influence

A frequent challenge to international agency personnel is that they have to relate to both positive and negative actions and developments. How do you try to check negative actions and at the same time encourage positive change? Let us look at one example, and imagine that a local police commander may be linked to all the acts listed in Table 5.2.

You may have to relate to all these acts. Our presentation is split into two. First we address the issue of how to follow up on positive signs of change. Then we look at the challenge of cracking down on negative acts to see whether such interventions may be combined with positive influence.

Positive response to positive change

Remember that a change of attitude may take time

Normally one must expect to exert influence for an extended period, with repeated reinforcement, confirmation and expansion of good commitments. How do you do this?

Keep in touch

Don't give your counterpart the possibility of forgetting what you expect from him. Paying a courtesy visit may be a valuable reminder of your positive expectations and a reinforcement of the contact, even if you don't raise any particular issues. Also remember that, in general, it is easier to like the people we see frequently. Use the contact to confirm and expand the positive expectations.

Don't forget to give positive feedback for positive acts or developments

Commend the person in question. Tell her about possible appreciation from others, about favourable reports, etc. In the same way as one can utilise statements,

Table 5.2 Positive and negative acts

Positive acts	*Negative acts*
Absence of abuse	Abuse
Reactions against abuse	No reaction against abuse
Protection	Ignoring the need for protection
Processing complaints	Ignoring complaints

positive acts can be used to reinforce positive roles. The approach is, in other words, to give a positive response to positive action and to let your counterpart understand that these are the sort of acts you expect.

NB If you have achieved a positive result and your service is nearing its end, you must do what you can to have your successor and others continue the positive influence.

Response to negative acts

Part of your mandate may be to respond to negative acts. It is not possible to give a complete blueprint for this. You may, however, have to raise negative incidents with the person you are trying to influence positively, and this may call for some advice.

If you want a positive development to continue, it is important that your counterpart remains in a positive role. 'Give a dog a bad name' is a well-known saying. If your counterpart is being blamed for negative developments or incidents, he may easily abandon his positive role. Possibilities of constructive development may thus be lost. A possible way to avoid this is to discuss negative incidents as events that have happened despite his attitude. He will thus save face, and may maintain whatever positive image has been established. Much depends on the choice of words.

Let us look at some alternative approaches that can be used to preserve a positive development, and at the same time crack down on what is negative. Let us assume you meet a political leader in a situation where, despite some positive developments, you have received reports of abuse carried out by her supporters. Here are some reactions you may express:

- We have received some negative reports that we believe you are going to take seriously.
- We are confident that you wish to do something about this.
- What measures do you think must be taken to avoid similar incidents?
- Do you think your efforts will be sufficient?
- How can we support you in this?
- We assume we can tell the victims that you will do your utmost to resolve the case?
- We must, as you know, report this, but we need close cooperation with you with a view to reporting on your follow-up and measures to prevent any recurrence.
- What can be done to give people a better impression of you and your supporters?
- Can you come with us and meet the victims (or complainants), so that they may give you their story, and perhaps you can tell them how you can improve their security in the future?
- Can we meet to discuss follow-up next Thursday?

Common to all these approaches is that they assume a positive engagement from your counterpart. If this works, she will commit herself to positive action. Every positive position from her side should be pinned down with recognition and agreement. Again, remember the advice about concluding a meeting: sum up what you have agreed on, and underline it with a firm handshake and eye contact.

It may of course happen that despite your efforts your counterpart commits serious and indisputable crimes, rendering it artificial to talk about a positive attitude or development. In this case, reporting or intervention by UN forces or police may perhaps be the only relevant measures. This will be the exception, however, compared to the many contexts where influence may be exerted by peaceful means. We shall revert to certain problems related to criticism as a means of influence (p. 85).

Back to Velika Kladusa

Let us now take a look at the challenge the UNHCR's protection staff faced in north-western Bosnia (p. 59). What techniques were used? The starting point of the process was the statement by the local police commander, who gave a positive picture of his own role, as one would expect.

- His positive statements were supported, and he was helped to reinforce them through discussions of related issues.
- He was told that other organisations had been informed about his statements.
- He was asked for practical assistance and cooperation.
- He got to know that vulnerable groups were informed about his attempts to protect them.
- He got a positive response to positive efforts.
- Negative incidents were raised with the expectation of positive action/improvement.
- The UNHCR officers tried to communicate by using active listening, respect and understanding. They would give agreement whenever justified.
- They were clear on their own mandate and expected respect for it.
- They did not conceal the fact that the UNHCR has expertise in human rights.
- They tried to progress in small steps, in order to ensure a yes to their requests for help or cooperation.
- Due to cooperation and positive response there were elements of sympathy in the interaction.
- They tried to follow up the contact over time.

The astute reader may have observed that the interaction probably included the influence of:

- role expectations and commitments
- role-play

- cognitive dissonance
- the 'yes' technique
- need fulfilment in communication
- authority
- expertise
- sympathy
- reciprocation.

Alongside meetings with the police, the UNHCR and the OSCE developed a series of seminars for police officers, discussing the work and challenges of policing in a democracy, in the light of human rights and socio-political developments in Bosnia. This contributed to confidence-building and facilitated cooperation.

Negative factors

Expectations of influence

If you call on someone who knows that you want to influence them, you should be prepared for difficulties. We have earlier highlighted our need for consistency. This means we prefer to stick to our positions, particularly the ones we have displayed through actions or statements. We need respect for what we stand for. If we are aware that someone is trying to have us change position, we are inclined to react negatively. This is one of the reasons why it is important to avoid raising problems and expressing criticism in the first meeting. It is important that your counterpart feels that you are not trying to influence him, and that your aim is cooperation on joint goals.

Negative expectations and acts

Just as positive influence may help someone develop a positive role, negative influence may lead to a negative role. If the police commander mentioned above is surrounded by people who expect him to commit abuses or create terror, they will influence him. If the expectations come from people or groups he is closely attached to or respects, the influence will be stronger yet. One cannot safeguard against this. But if he has any idea of abuse and terror being an ethical problem, then the good role may appear more attractive. Even so, if you want to influence a person closely connected to a group, it may be necessary to approach the group or selected members of it as well.

Like negative expectations, negative acts also influence us. Any act of terror or abuse or other negative behaviour will influence the perpetrator, and thus be a step backwards. But if you, as suggested earlier, can put a temporary halt to the negative deeds through active follow-up while the person in question fulfils a good role, then positive influence will result.

Difficult personalities

What if a person is downright evil or sadistic, or has some other personality problem? Research has shown that, in general, we overestimate the significance of personality traits as determining behaviour. Statements such as 'He is just hopeless' or 'only evil' are normally baseless. While there are some particularly difficult personalities, our social environment generally has great influence on our choice of action. In addition, no one is only evil. Many of the staff participating in the extermination of Jews during the Second World War were good fathers or mothers. Again, it depends on what kind of roles and situations we find ourselves in.

In 1993 the psychologists Lee Ross and Steven Samuels conducted the following experiment at Stanford University, US (Aronson *et al.*, 1999): They selected two groups of students, based on the criteria competitive/cooperative. One group was selected among students who the resident assistants considered to be especially cooperative, the other was picked among students termed highly competitive.

They told half the participants that the name of the game they were to play was the Wall Street Game, and the other half that it was the Community Game.

The name of the game turned out to make a considerable difference. Of those told it was the Wall Street Game, two-thirds played competitively, with little difference between the players assumed to be competitive and the others. Among those told it was the Community Game, two-thirds chose a cooperative approach, and the players assumed to be competitive were just as cooperative as the others.

The techniques we have described are also effective when dealing with difficult personalities. Our desire to be considered positively by others makes us prone to influence by social norms, role expectations and role-plays. Due to our desire to be consistent, we are influenced by the yes technique and by cognitive dissonance. We all need to be treated with respect, understanding and recognition, and communication addressing such needs is therefore likely to influence us.

A particularly difficult person may have qualities that make him less accessible to influence in some contexts, but also more vulnerable in others. This issue cannot be discussed in depth here, but in general difficult persons cannot escape influence.

Traditional approaches

Many of the techniques of influence described above are apparently not much used in conflict interventions and may perhaps, as earlier observed, never have been used systematically. Some other methods are quite frequently used, and we shall take a closer look at them.

Persuasion

Without trying to give it a precise definition, we may describe persuasion as a mixture of approaches, where logical argument is essential, but in combination with evaluations, suggestions and various psychological influencing techniques.

We shall not discuss this subject in depth, and it may not be possible to give an accurate guide to good persuasion. We focus here on the logical argumentation for a position. In doing so, we may benefit from a brief summary of research and theory from social psychology.

- It is difficult to persuade others when an attempt to do so is expected.
- A trustworthy person or an expert convinces us more easily than others.
- An attractive person (physically or personally) convinces more easily than others.
- If one's own arguments are convincing, one is best served by including the counter-arguments in one's presentation.
- The more personally relevant the message is to us, the more inclined we are to listen to its contents.
- If the message has no personal relevance to us, we will be more influenced by external factors such as form of presentation and the qualities of the speaker.
- Lasting change of attitude is more likely where persuasion happens as a result of logical argument rather than through external factors.
- A person in a good mood may be accommodating, but focuses less on the content of an argument.

Applied to our context, this suggests the following:

- Don't let your counterpart feel that you are out to persuade her. As observed earlier, we are apt to put up resistance to persuasion, since this normally assumes a conscious change of attitude and an appreciation that we were wrong.
- If you expect to be able to convince your counterpart, try to find an approach that makes the issue relevant to her personally.
- If you can defeat the counter-arguments, discuss them in your presentation.
- The form of the presentation and external factors become important when the subject is not of personal interest.
- Don't expect a lasting change of attitude if you have succeeded in impressing or scaring your counterpart into accepting your view, or if he does so just because he is in a good mood.

Applied to your interventions in conflict, the first point will probably make persuasion the exception rather than the rule.

Value judgements: praise and criticism

We often seek to influence conflicts by making value judgements. These may be moral, ethical, legal, etc. You may, for instance, tell a representative of a group that their acts are evil or good, destructive or constructive, acceptable or unacceptable. Let us take a closer look at two very common kinds of value judgement, expressed through criticism and praise.

Criticism hampers influence

Criticism is sometimes expressed to expose a position or a view to a counterpart or to the world. To this end, criticism may serve a purpose. However, if the objective is positive change, criticism becomes problematic. Even justified criticism tends to arouse a negative reaction, and may therefore be counterproductive.

Our need for a positive self-image makes criticism as such unpleasant, easily provoking defensive reactions. Accepting criticism in a relaxed way demands more balance and self-knowledge than most of us have. We are less able to take criticism from strangers than from someone we know and trust. In the presence of others or in public, we become even more vulnerable. In such cases our self-image as well as our ideas of how others see us are threatened.

It does, of course, happen that we abide by criticism because the logic or ethics of the message convinces us. Other factors which increase the chances of criticism succeeding are a desire to cooperate or to achieve something, the possibility of recognition or respect[3] and the fear of negative consequences. Social expectations and roles as well as authority, expertise, sympathy and friendship are also significant. Still, criticism will normally arouse negative reactions, particularly in case of conflict. Unless we find criticism justified, we will only comply if our wish to avoid the criticism or the consequences is stronger than our negative reaction. This is similar to our reaction to threats (p. 89). If not, the person expressing the criticism will be left with the negative reaction as the only outcome.

When intervening in a conflict you can rarely count on the desire to avoid criticism. There is, however, a clear risk that you may be less liked after having raised the criticism. This does not mean one can avoid criticism completely, but it is important to remember what effect it has on the recipient.

How to express criticism

While performing your assignment, you may often have to react to negative events. The usual way to criticise is to characterise something as negative. As observed above, if the purpose is positive change and not just to state your view, such an approach is problematic.

You have two possibilities. Let us suppose that a political leader has access to a local radio station partly funded by your organisation. He has used it for agitation against a vulnerable group, and you wish to prevent this from happening again. You may, in principle, choose between the following alternatives.

EXPRESS YOUR NEGATIVE VIEW

You may say that the agitation is unethical or illegal and demand that the unacceptable programmes stop. The militia leader will most likely disagree with your assessment. You should then expect a counter-reaction, and he will only comply if his wish to avoid the criticism or the consequences is stronger than his counter-reaction.

ADDRESS A POSITIVE CHANGE

You may, for example, say that there is a need to develop the profile of the radio programmes in such a way that all groups feel respected, and ask the militia leader if he can commit himself to ensuring the change. You may perhaps refer to earlier balanced broadcasts on the same channel and suggest that this is the tone that should prevail. The criticism will, in this case, be latent as you are focusing on the solution. This approach also puts the message across without rubbing in the negative aspect.

The point is that it is easier for us to accept a positive change that is not necessitated by our bad behaviour. In a way we escape criticism by accepting change. (This is also a factor in 'Shortcuts to resolution', p. 166.) We shall not try to present a complete guide to how to express criticism, but depending on your relationship with your counterpart and the purpose of the criticism, it may be wise to spend a little time contemplating your choice of approach. You might find it appropriate to focus directly on positive change.

Should you give your counterpart a way out?

Sometimes it may be tempting to label a counterpart clearly, removing any doubt about his deplorable acts or qualities. Clear and direct speech may also be required at times, for instance in cases of serious human rights abuse. But if your purpose is positive change, you might consider giving your counterpart a chance to save face. He may wish to explain his action. If he is allowed to do so, he may find it easier to move towards positive change, and as human rights defenders we should give everyone the chance of self-defence. The fact that you may disagree strongly with what he says is another matter. If you make a counterpart feel like a rat in a trap, he is not likely ever to cooperate with you.

Praise makes it easier

Positive judgements have a strong potential for influence. Our need for a positive self-image makes us very susceptible to positive reactions from others. We normally accept praise, flattery and appreciation without much objection.

Joe Girard of the US, termed the best car salesman in the world by the *Guinness Book of Records*, had the habit of sending postcards to some 13,000 customers every month, simply saying 'I like you' (Cialdini, 1993).

Some psychological experiments indicate that we like the people who flatter us even if we know that their praise is not justified. (But others indicate that it may backfire if we feel manipulated.) This human weakness is one of the reasons why positive response to positive action is so effective. Praise makes us feel comfortable, and a role that brings appreciation is attractive. Thus, we like those praising us and are inclined to heed what they say. As we have suggested above, give a positive response to every positive act. But remember, it should come naturally.

Requests and suggestions

These means of intervention span a vast spectrum. They vary with the strength of the imperative (demand/order) expressed through them, from the mild and cautious phrased as a polite question, to what we would term a demand. How far do they work?

Requests or suggestions coherent with the recipient's wish are not a problem unless they are perceived as untimely interference. More problematic are the ones that contradict the recipient's wish, typically when suggesting a change. These may easily be perceived as criticism and thus something negative and provoking. Often there will also be a fear of losing face if complying. The stronger the imperative, the more resistance there is.

According to reactance theory (Brehm, 1966), we react negatively when we feel that our freedom of choice is threatened. This evokes an uncomfortable emotional reaction that we may lessen by acting contrary to the suggestion.

In an experiment in 1976, two types of boards were put up in the toilets of the student campus at a US university. One of them read: 'Do not write on the walls under any circumstances!' The other: 'Please do not write on the walls.' Two weeks later considerably more had been written on the walls where the strong statement had been made (Pennebaker and Sanders, 1976).

The students clearly disliked being dictated to. The chances of compliance increase with the same factors that pertain to criticism. The situation may also be such that strong requests or suggestions are the only means available, for instance in an acute crisis, where you just have to try.

During Operation Storm in the former Yugoslavia in 1995, a very dangerous situation developed as a convoy of Serbian refugees was to leave the Topusco area of Croatia. Among the refugees there were also Serbian soldiers and war material, and Croatian forces advanced rapidly towards the convoy. The UN forces expected an artillery attack, but had no means to prevent it. A colonel from the UN forces went to see the Croatian commander, accompanied by a liaison officer, a representative of the UN police and a protection officer from the UNHCR. Together they made a strong appeal to the commander to refrain from attacking. After hectic negotiations, including disarming the Serbian soldiers, the Croats accepted the appeal, and hundreds of people were saved.

In this case moral and personal authority may have prevailed. These are not factors one can always count on. Other than in acute situations, you should normally try other forms of influence first. Also, beware of the dangers of a suggestion that is rejected. The section on cognitive dissonance (pp. 66–68) explained that what we do influences us. If you get a no in response to a pressing request, the person who rejected you may unconsciously perceive this as a negative act towards you. The consequence is that she will probably like you less afterwards, and that her need for consistency is likely to make her turn down your requests in the future. On the other hand, if you get an acceptance, you will more easily get a yes from the same person later.

Demands

The focus here is on demands that behaviour be changed or maintained, or that a certain act be performed or refrained from. Both are problematic approaches to conflict. The stronger the demand, the more likely we are to get a counter-reaction. The likelihood is stronger here than with requests and suggestions. Demands may, of course, be supported by other social influences. And if you can put power behind the demand, this may be decisive. Remember, however, that a negative reaction is normally inevitable, and that future cooperation may be impossible. In general, you should only express demands when you cannot influence your counterpart by other means, and when it is impossible to succeed with requests or suggestions.

Threats and sanctions

Threats

Threats are, alas, a very common means in international conflict management. They imply that bad or negative consequences will befall the addressee if the demand is not accepted. These may range from a delegate's statement that something will be reported to a state leader's warning of international sanctions or military intervention. Threats may be dictating, for example: 'If you don't sign this agreement, we will use sanctions.' They may also be aversive, for example: 'If you do enter the area, we are going to open fire.'

A dictating threat will normally be perceived as a provocation, and, subject to the situation, may be a dangerous means in conflict contexts. An aversive threat may also be seen as provocative, but normally to a lesser degree. Psychological research indicates that threats are generally not appropriate for solving conflicts, because they impede confidence-building between the parties. This means that threats should not be used if we wish to build confidence and facilitate cooperation. As long as we hope for peaceful solutions to a conflict, threats are a risky approach. But what if there is no more hope of a peaceful solution? If it is going to work, the sanction must outweigh the counter-reaction. Let us use an example where you have credible force at hand.

You get to know that a militia group is planning to intercept a convoy carrying provisions meant for a refugee camp run by your organisation. They maintain that their own villages get less support than others, despite evident needs. You tell the group's leader that you will have to ask the UN forces to intervene if they don't abandon their plans. The leader will normally only refrain if his wish to avoid the UN intervention outweighs his feeling of being provoked by the threat.

This picture may be compared with criticism and demands. Unless the threatened evil outweighs his negative reaction, the outcome will be contrary to what was hoped for, meaning that the threat will provoke a counter-reaction to the one threatening as well as his position or message. And should the threats lead to compliance, the negative attitude is apt to be reinforced by the humiliation experienced. This means that the counterpart will normally defy your threat the moment it ceases to be heavy enough. If, for example, militants are forced to leave a minority group in peace, one must expect this group to be harassed even more the moment the threat ceases. Remember reactance theory (p. 88): this problem is constantly being illustrated in international politics.

Are threats required?

To protect peace and human lives, international organisations may at times have to use threats. The militia's plans to intercept a convoy, mentioned above, is one such example. In that case, however, the threat serves to avert an acute crisis, not to solve a conflict. The militia group believed that their own villages did not get a fair share of humanitarian support. If this is a problem you wish to solve, other initiatives are required. One way is to combine the threat with a softer approach. You may for instance say, 'We must alert the UN forces if you start approaching our convoy, but we are aware of your opinion on distribution of humanitarian support, and we would like to meet you to hear you out.' In this case your offer to meet may start a process towards a solution, whereas the threat serves to stop a dangerous development.

Can negative consequences be used without being threatening?

One must not forget that balancing negative consequences against positive ones is part of daily life. If you draw attention to possible negative consequences without being provocative, you may be able to utilise this in conflict contexts without coming across as threatening. The wording means a lot.

If you state, 'We will abandon the road project unless you improve the security in the area', this will be perceived as a threat made by you and your agency. You might, however, choose to say, 'We are worried about our road project, that we absolutely wish to continue, but security is a problem. My agency has found that we will have to stop the project unless security is improved, and we hope you can help us avoid this.'

The practical message is the same, but in the last case you sympathise with your counterpart, and depict the negative consequences as an undesired evil. By combining this with a friendly appeal, and implying a positive role for your counterpart, you increase the chances of avoiding provocation. If so, you increase the possibilities that the 'threat', combined with the positive influence, will have a motivating effect.

Reporting

A practical situation where the threat perspective is relevant is reporting on negative incidents. Local actors often perceive reports as an evil that international delegates use to get what they want. You can angle this differently.

For example, in a meeting with the local mayor you might say:

> As you may know, I am obliged to report to our head office, which again reports to the regional centre (possibly to the countries involved). I would like to make positive reports for this area. To do so I need positive and open cooperation with you. And in this regard I hope that you and I together may go through any negative report that comes in. If so, I will be able to report what you do to solve the problems. If we agree on this, our cooperation could be the subject of my first report.

Sanctions

Civilian sanctions in various forms may be a practical follow-up to threats, but are also used to mark political reactions to or positions on an incident or development. As a means for positive change, sanctions rarely have the desired effect.

Eric Thomas, spokesman for American industry's anti-sanctions campaign, contended in 1998 that more than half the earth's population were living in countries subjected to sanctions by the US. And the proportion would increase to two-thirds if sanctions proposed or under preparation were included (*Aftenposten*, 8 April 1998).

These sanctions did not generally give the desired results. The reason probably lies in the strong counter-reactions that sanctions inevitably cause. If sanctions follow threats, they provoke all the threats' negative reactions, but in addition even stronger antipathy, aggression and bitterness.

One may also point out cases where sanctions have seemed to work. The economic restrictions against South Africa are possibly one example. The point is, however, that sanctions normally come with a high price. In Iraq, the UN-imposed sanctions led to disastrous effects for the civilian population while failing to achieve the level of compliance from the government that the UN regarded as necessary. As a means of conflict intervention, sanctions should therefore never be used without a prior critical and profound assessment.

Promises

Promises are often part of the classical stick and carrot approach, where threats and punishment alternate with promises and rewards. The promises we focus on here imply benefits to a counterpart if he acts in a certain way. This may have dangerous effects. Our counterpart may easily adopt a role where he does the right thing not because he wishes to, but because he is being rewarded. Unless the reward is insignificant, it may become an important motive. If this is repeated, progress may be impeded: 'I want compensation, otherwise no cooperation.' Such trade-off may reduce your counterpart's respect for you.

If you wish to help a person shift to a positive role, it is counterproductive to buy her cooperation first. The recipient may also be inspired to try to achieve more rewards for cooperating. International delegates and high level politicians sometimes offer a more subtle kind of reward, terming possible benefits as 'natural parts of constructive cooperation' without attaching specific conditions to the benefits. It is, however, important to remember that if the reward is the motive for the act we will not achieve positive attitude change. The US may have been caught up in such a pattern of rewards in its handling of the conflict between Israel and the Palestinians (Pruitt and Rubin, 1986). The US efforts in Afghanistan to win hearts and minds through various kinds of financial support provide another contentious example.

Summing up: effects of traditional approaches

Traditional approaches to intervention vis-à-vis one party to a conflict are problematic to a large extent.

- Persuasion is problematic because people don't want to be persuaded. It only works under certain conditions.
- Criticism and negative evaluations often provoke counter-reactions. (Praise and flattery normally have the opposite effect and arouse positive feelings.)
- Requests and suggestions often arouse negative reactions.
- Threats provoke and impede confidence-building.
- Sanctions evoke strong negative reactions.
- Promises and rewards may provide the 'wrong' motivation instead of a positive change of attitude.

Notes

1 Some observers maintained that the Taliban's crackdown on opium in the early days of its reign in Afghanistan was largely ignored by the international community, whereas criticism of human rights violations was rife. Arguably this represented a lost opportunity for dialogue.
2 Others call it 'Door in the face'. See Cialdini (1993) and Aronson *et al.* (1999).
3 Subject to the circumstances, accepting criticism may also be seen as mature or brave.

References

Aronson, E., Wilson, T. D. and Akert, R. M. (1999) *Social Psychology*, New York: Addison-Wesley Longman.

Brehm, J. W. (1966) *A Theory of Psychological Reactance*, New York: Academic Press.

Cialdini, R. (1993) *Influence. Science and practice*, New York: Harper Collins.

Pennebaker J. and Sanders, D. (1976) 'American graffiti, effects of authority and reactance arousal', *Personality and Social Psychology Bulletin* 2: 264–267.

Pruitt, D. G. and Rubin, J. Z. (1986) *Social Conflict, Escalation, Stalemate and Settlement*, New York: Random House.

Rosenberg, M. B. (1999) *Nonviolent Communication. A Language of Compassion*, Del Mar, CA: Puddle Dancer Press.

Viswesvaran, C. and Deshpande, S. P. (1996) 'Ethics, success, and job satisfaction: a test of dissonance theory in India', *Journal of Business Ethics*, 15(10): 1065–1069.

Woodhouse, T. and Duffey, T. (2009) *Peacekeeping and International Conflict Resolution*, www.peaceopstraining.org/courses/peacekeeping-and-international-conflict-resolution/.

Zimbardo P. G. and Leippe, M. R. (1991) *The Psychology of Attitude Change and Social Influence*, New York: McGraw-Hill.

6 Peacebuilding

In August 1999 East Timor decided in a UN-supported referendum to break away from Indonesia, after 25 years of occupation. Indonesia-friendly militias responded with massive violence and destruction. The Indonesian army supported the attacks, which forced some 250,000 people to flee their homes. After a negotiated withdrawal of the Indonesian army and deployment of international peacekeeping forces, the international community made a comprehensive effort to build peace in the country. The UN and the World Bank, supported by 50 international donors, contributed US$4 billion. East Timor subsequently gained independence in 2002, and with external threats gone, the new country was relatively peaceful for three years and the peacebuilding was widely considered to be a success. The international community began to withdraw its support and the UN reduced its presence early on. In April/May 2006 internal violence broke out, causing at least 32 deaths and driving some 150,000 people from their homes. A breakdown of the government ensued, and international forces were again brought in. The UN's first effort to build a state from scratch had failed.

The East Timor case illustrates the complexity of peacebuilding, and research from the years following the crises has provided a number of interesting lessons we draw upon in this chapter.

The challenge

War-ravaged countries are in a precarious state. The government and judiciary may be dysfunctional, the police and the military are often out of control and abusive. Private institutions and organisations are generally weak. The normal economy ceases to function while a war economy prevails. Human rights are often abused and various aspects of civil life such as health services, education and employment are badly affected. There may be a host of unresolved conflicts between various groups, some at a local level, others nationwide, threatening national stability. Different ethnic, religious or political groups may use the transition phase to seek influence. There are typically a lot of arms held by ex-combatants who have few work prospects, and communities may be reluctant to reintegrate them. The government may want peace but also impunity for its own violent supporters, and has little knowledge of peacebuilding. How do we progress from this state to one where peace is at least likely?

This chapter discusses peacebuilding concepts and parameters and offers advice on defining our role in a peacebuilding perspective. It discusses government and UN responsibilities and practices. In addition to leadership at different levels, it addresses planning, analysis and identification of interests and needs. The requirements of effective implementation are discussed, including identification of implementing actors, effective coordination and monitoring.

Reconciliation is a major element in peacebuilding but is often neglected by both the international community and the responsible government. This chapter discusses different reconciliation approaches, including a model from social psychology on how cooperation between adversaries can be used to break down antagonism.

Even if you are not directly involved in peacebuilding but, for instance, are providing emergency assistance to people in a conflict area, you need to observe that your action has indirect effects on peace, and advice is offered to this end.

You may recall that we have given peacebuilding a broad definition, as we include all non-violent efforts appropriate to move societies and human relationships towards peace, harmony and positive interaction (see p. 8).

Building peace may be about a special activity or programme, or imply full-scale statebuilding, nationbuilding and conflict resolution/reconciliation. As conflict resolution mechanisms like mediation have been dealt with earlier, these are not included in this chapter.

As mentioned in the Introduction, this book aims at bridging a gap between academia and practitioners. While many of the books on offer may be too comprehensive and theoretical for practical use in the field, there are a range of documents that take a more practical approach to peacebuilding.

These include strategic documents and guidelines published by different peacebuilding actors. Documents developed by the World Bank, EU, OECD/DAC, G7+ and OSCE were mentioned in Chapter 2. Useful publications on various peacebuilding aspects have also been produced by a number of national agencies. Examples are:

Vaux, Goodhand and Walker (2002) *Conducting Conflict Assessments. Guidance Notes*, DFID;

Brounéus (2003) *Reconciliation – Theory and Practice for Development Cooperation*, SIDA;

NORAD (2004) *Peacebuilding: A Development Perspective: Strategic Framework*;

Australian Aid (2011) *Framework for Working in Fragile and Conflict-affected States*;

USAID's range of '*technical publications on conflict management and mitigation*'.[1]

Adding to the insights of such documents are:

Woodhouse and Duffey (2009) *Peacekeeping and International Conflict Resolution*;

UN Peace Operations Training Institute's curriculum for on-line training (2009);

de Coning and de Carvalho (2013) *Peacebuilding Handbook*, which is based on African research and training.

A matter of interests and needs

Peacebuilding is basically about addressing identified interests and needs, not in a narrow sense as something people necessarily crave, but deriving from the overall need for peace and what is needed to achieve it. The interests may be physical, such as the needs for food, shelter, security and compensation. Others may be emotionally based, such as peace of mind, respect, understanding and justice.

Some interests relate to factors that build positive relations and a harmonious society, and the peacebuilding challenge is to introduce or reinforce these factors. Examples are acess to reconciliation and appropriate mechanisms for conflict resolution, as well as employment and functioning public services.

Other interests relate to factors that sustain or breed conflict. Examples are revenge and exploitation. Peacebuilding requires efforts to remove or weaken these factors and the motivational drivers behind them, such as hate and mistrust.

Obstacles to interest fulfilment may be cultural, such as the caste system in India, or religious, such as the Shia/Sunni antagonism in parts of the Muslim world. They may also be systemic, such as the ethnic discrimination institutionalised between Malays and other groups in Malaysia, or the world-wide production and proliferation of arms. In peace/war contexts, there are normally a number of significant systems to observe. Under 'Common needs' (pp. 115–122) you will find that many interventions are about improving or restoring/building the systems of society.

Human rights

In our terminology, peacebuilding needs include human rights. The extent to which we pursue them as rights or as needs may vary. One may have to stand up for the right to life and a fair trial, while access to work and social security might more naturally be addressed as needs.

Some peacebuilding actors suggest that human rights should be the basis of peacebuilding.[2] If we assume that there are clearly defined human rights that correspond with everything needed to build peace, this approach is logically unproblematic. However, some peacebuilding needs fall outside the human rights realm. The need for reconciliation is one such example, and it is difficult to decide to what extent livelihood improvement, one of the New Deal goals mentioned below, is a human right.

So our approach is that peacebuilding indeed implies the pursuit of human rights, but also needs outside this realm.

Fragile states and the New Deal

The World Bank's report on conflict, security and development (2011) offered striking data on the relationship between conflicts, crime and development, showing that fragile and conflict-affected states (FCS) were lagging far behind other developing countries in terms of poverty reduction and fulfilment of the Millennium Development Goals.[3]

The report called for increased attention to the needs of such states and, as mentioned earlier, in December 2011 the G7+, the group of then 17 fragile states, and international partners, gathered at the Fourth High Level Forum on Aid Effectiveness in Busan, South Korea, adopted a new framework for dealing with FCS. *The New Deal* calls on the international community to render more consistent support to FCS, and suggests five specific peace and statebuilding goals:

- Legitimate politics: foster inclusive political settlements and conflict resolution.
- Security: establish and strengthen people's security.
- Justice: address injustices and increase people's access to justice.
- Economic foundations: generate employment and improve livelihoods.
- Revenues and services: manage revenue and build capacity for accountable and fair service delivery.

While these broadly formulated and generally adequate goals would cover most peacebuilding needs, our approach here is different. This chapter focuses on identification of the specific needs of a country or region as the basis for peacebuilding. To identify these needs, a comprehensive needs analysis is proposed, and this analysis should serve as a basis for peacebuilding plans. If so, the need for external standardised objectives is not obvious.[4] Specific country plans may also deviate from the New Deal objectives. Reconciliation, an important but often neglected need, is not part of the objectives. Neither was reconciliation included in an early version of indicators for the New Deal goals, presented by the International Dialogue on Peacebuilding and Statebuilding in April 2013.[5]

Reconciliation

Reconciliation, defined on p. 7, is an essential peacebuilding element. Reconciling adversaries is a prime need if they are to go on living together after a violent conflict, and both victims and perpetrators of violence may need reconciliation for their personal healing process.

Unfortunately this need is often neglected, both by the responsible government and the international community. This chapter discusses reconciliation perspectives in a number of contexts, and addresses practical approaches under 'The need for conflict resolution and reconciliation' (pp. 122–125).

A function of time or influence

The human mind normally develops a distance from the past. Europe today shows little of the hatred and resentment that marked countries and people after the Second World War. This has to do with changing generations but also with our ability to reconcile ourselves with the past. For the individual, however, reconciliation is highly dependent on the seriousness of the wounds. Persons exposed to atrocities may never wish to be reconciled.

Influence for reconciliation may come from others, for instance through role expectations (p. 60). It may come from within ourselves as a consequence of our acts and thoughts. Often both factors work simultaneously.

The influence is most likely to emerge when hostilities have ceased, but we may find elements of reconciliation even at the peak of conflicts. The mediation processes we have described above would, if successfully implemented, include elements of reconciliation for the people involved. Mediation or negotiations may in fact be the beginning of a wider reconciliation process.

Reconciliation may take place as a result of insight and understanding of the other party's acts and motives, but we may also come to be reconciled with former enemies without necessarily understanding them.

As peacebuilders cannot wait for reconciliation to develop over time, we are going to discuss reconciliation as a structured process.

The time perspective

Urgent issues

Some peacebuilding aspects must be addressed early on. Security is normally an urgent need, and clean water, sanitation, food and shelter are essential components of early recovery.

After a war there may be a large number of former fighters, normally young men, who find themselves idle. There is a need to disarm them, reintegrate them and get them involved in gainful activities as soon as possible. Whatever long-term plans are being developed, such issues cannot wait. This is not just about preventing violence. A fair degree of security may help overcome mistrust and increase the likelihood of cooperation. Disarmament and reintegration are one example; for the process to succeed, both the civilians and the combatants affected need to believe in it.

After the Aceh peace agreement in 2005, substantial funds were set aside for compensation to former fighters and victims. However, two years after the identification process started, the funds had only partially been disbursed. Although the disarmament process appeared to be successful, there were reports of a steady rise in violent crime.

There will be many groups and individuals who wish to have a say in a country's or region's future development. These could be resistance groups, political parties, NGOs, religious communities, etc. It is important that such actors should have a sense of inclusion and respect as early as possible. This means that there is normally a need for early dialogue, peace conferences and establishment of forums where they all get a say: see 'The need for conflict resolution and reconciliation', (pp. 122–125).

A major challenge in this regard is the need for vertical integration. Peace and stability are more likely if the poor, the middle class and the elites all participate in the choice of direction. The all-too-common exclusion of non-elites and the concentration of power/resources in the hands of small groups may work for a while, but are likely to threaten long-term stability. Peacebuilders should promote an understanding of this perspective.[6]

Long-term perspectives

'It took the 20 fastest-moving countries an average of 17 years to get the military out of politics, 20 years to achieve functioning bureaucratic quality, and 27 years to bring corruption under reasonable control' (World Bank, 2011: 108, discussing basic governance transformations in the twentieth century).[7]

How do we relate practically to such daunting perspectives? UN peacebuilding missions have habitually been given one-year mandates. After a one-year extension, another UN mission normally takes over, with many of the same core staff, but a revised mandate. While some UN engagements go on for many years, the changing mandates have often reflected early scaling down. There may be pressure from UN members to complete operations even if there are indications that many problems still need to be addressed. East Timor was such an example (Ofstad, 2012).

The time limit on mandates and early scaling down are probably related to the political economy of the international community as well as democratic competition, the NGO funding cycle and other factors. Obviously a one-year mandate is artificial when we are aware that sustained efforts will be needed for many years. One may hope, however, that the mandate of the UN mission to the Republic of South Sudan (UNMISS) established on 9 July 2011 signals a movement towards longer commitments. This mandate applies the usual one-year time-frame, but with the expressed 'intention to renew for further periods as may be required' (Security Council Resolution 1996, 2011: 3).

There are also other indications that we have begun to take the time perspective more seriously. The new UN peacebuilding architecture introduced in 2006 (p. 105) aims to support the countries found eligible till 'foundations for sustainable peace and development are established, or upon the request by national authorities of the country under consideration' (Security Council Resolution 1645: 5). (One must observe, however, that these institutions have no operational mandate.)

Moreover, UN country teams and resident coordinators are trying to ensure continuity in their work. The UN Development Programme (UNDP) and specialised UN agencies may contribute to a variety of sustained peacebuilding efforts. Some countries have started providing longer-term funding for NGOs, and the World Bank has declared its intention to work towards ensuring that essential institutions in fragile and conflict-affected states 'receive sustained support over several years'.[8]

Fortunately, not all peacebuilding activities take a long time. Physical reconstruction may happen fast. So may training and even the establishment of new institutions. What about conflict resolution and reconciliation? Old foes are sometimes reconciled quickly. This may happen through misunderstandings being cleared up, through confession and forgiveness or through constructive interaction/cooperation. The South African Truth and Reconciliation Commission apparently achieved some strikingly good and immediate results, even though dealing with old and deep conflicts.

Let us say your agency has got a time perspective of two–three years. You may still be able to make a difference, perhaps even to a large number of people. One challenge may be to define activities that work within the time you have available. It is our obligation to keep this perspective in mind and to make our peacebuilding efforts as time-effective as possible.

Sustainability

This is an essential issue both at national and at local level. If the effects are meant to be long term, the local society must be able to take over when the programme ends. Programmes that end in collapse are frustrating and counterproductive.

If your agency is committed for three years and supports the judiciary by funding judges, you need to be sure that the government or someone else will fund them when the three years are over. Depriving people of something you have given them might be worse than not giving it at all. One should normally not be overly optimistic about a war-torn society's ability to take over such projects. If they are essential to peace, the international community might have to continue to support them for many years.

There are activities that local actors may take over within a relatively short time-span, however. Small-scale saving and credit projects are examples. To identify such possibilities, you have to assess carefully the local society's resources. If in serious doubt about a project's sustainability, you should drop it.

Your role in peacebuilding

Micro, macro or indirect influence?

International personnel relate to peacebuilding in three different contexts. The micro level, where most of us become involved, spans a wide range of programme and project activities – from reconstruction of a public office to small-scale community reconciliation projects or vocational training in villages. There is in principle no limit to how micro-level projects might support peaceful development.

The macro level is about high-level leadership, planning, coordination and monitoring, ideally by a competent government, but often requiring strong support from the international community. Senior UN personnel may be involved in the design and planning process, as well as in implementation/high-level advice. Even if your work is at the micro level, it is important to have an understanding of macro-level perspectives, which are discussed in a number of contexts in this chapter.

Indirect influence may take place at both micro and macro level

All humanitarian and development aid activities have bearings on the development of society, including peace and conflict. A health or education project may have reconciling effects if it reaches all stakeholders, but it may also arouse envy if the benefits are not equally distributed. Many organisations working in conflict areas implement their projects without relating consciously to the conflict. They may unwittingly fuel tensions or contribute to a war economy. The possibility of indirect influence calls for a conscious approach, whatever your level of work (see 'Do no harm', p. 148).

International workers should be advocates for peace

Whether in a discussion with a local mayor or in a training session with a local community, you should represent peace values and try to spread positive 'rings in the water'. At the end of the day, peace is a matter of attitudes.

Choice of activities

Ideally peacebuilding should be an 'all out' approach, including all activities needed to promote stability and peaceful development. But as our resources and capacity are normally insufficient, we have to prioritise. We have previously (p. 16) observed that your agency's choices may be decided by its strategic frameworks, international instruments and norms, as well as different allegiances.

Within the scope of such frames, a sound norm is to focus on what we are doing best, meaning fields where we have competence and resources. But in a chaotic scene where everything seems to be needed, such norms are easily disregarded.

The reconstruction phase in Aceh after the 2004 tsunami saw a number of organisations involved in activities outside their realm of experience. One example was housing, where a large number of houses were rejected by local people because they lacked sanitary facilities.

The EU voluntary code of conduct for a better division of labour between the EU donors in developing countries is an effort to address this issue, for example, suggesting that 'EU donors should confine their assistance in a partner country to two sectors in which they offer the best comparative advantage' (EU, 2007). If you provide EU-funded aid in a conflict zone, these guidelines must inform your choice of peacebuilding activities.

Level of society

As we prioritise, a relevant question may be: on what level of society will our efforts be most effective? Jean Paul Lederach (1997: 39) depicts a society pyramid with three levels:

> **Level 1 Top leadership**
> Military/political/religious
> Leaders with high visibility
> **Level 2 Middle range leadership**
> Leaders in respected sectors
> Ethnic religious leaders
> Academics/intellectuals
> Humanitarian leaders (NGOs)
> **Level 3 Grassroots leadership**
> Local leaders
> Leaders of indigenous NGOs
> Community developers
> Local health officials
> Refugee camp leaders

Lederach observes a need for inclusion and coordination across all three levels, but suggests that the mid-level has the greatest potential for establishing an infrastructure for long-term peacebuilding. A common view is that the need for local cultures of peace suggests peacebuilding efforts from below (Curle 1996 and Ramsbotham *et al.*, 2011). Do these views offer the guidance you need?

In some societies major change is dependent on the top. Examples are dictatorships where precious little happens without top-level consent. One could hardly expect effective mid-level outreach to Milosevic in Serbia or Mugabe in Zimbabwe, and peacebuilding often takes place in countries with top-level power concentration. In other countries the grassroots level may hold the best potential for change. In Somaliland in Somalia, a breakdown of the political infrastructure in the early 1990s opened the way for constructive initiatives at the sub-clan level.

The level you address may of course depend on your organisation's profile or speciality, and the level that holds the best potential for influence may not be within your reach. But the point here is that a concrete assessment is needed, and it is our duty as peacebuilders to make it.

Geography

For leading actors such as the UN and the World Bank as well as regional development banks, embassies and specialised agencies working with a government, the country's capital or other central locations may be the natural operation base. However, we sometimes see central places being 'swarmed' by international organisations, while more vulnerable rural areas receive limited attention. Sadly, at times the desire to be visible seems to influence where organisations work. If we are serious about addressing needs, the following questions should be pertinent:

- Where do we find the greatest needs?
- Where can we best utilise our resources? This relates to our capacities, logistics, the possibilities of cooperation with local and international actors, support from peacekeeping forces, etc.
- How can we avoid sustaining front lines? Part of the peacebuilding challenge is to promote interaction across the front line.

It may be difficult to balance these different concerns. The point is that any organisation should make a conscious assessment, based on the knowledge and understanding they are able to attain. (Analysis of peacebuilding needs is discussed on p. 109.)

Whatever your conclusions as to what you should do, where and at what level, please remember to present your ideas and plans to the peacebuilding leadership and/or local government before you start in earnest. (See 'Identification of implementing actors', pp. 137–139.)

Peacebuilding leadership

Who should take the lead role?

Leadership is an essential macro issue. As in any complex endeavour, peacebuilding should be led by an actor who ensures strategic direction, adequate analysis and planning, effective implementation and coordination as well as monitoring and adjustments.

Any legitimate government has the right and responsibility to lead peacebuilding efforts in its own country. However, after a war or violent conflict there may be a power vacuum. The government may be shattered or dysfunctional. In some cases, such as when a region achieves independence, there may be no government at all. In such cases, a state may have to be built from scratch, including all the institutions and structures required. In cases where the government has been a party to a conflict, it may not be trusted by other parties to lead the peace process. But as long as its right to rule a territory remains undisputed, it will always be for the government to decide whether it wants to cede leadership responsibilities.

If the government cannot or does not want to take a lead, the UN would be a natural alternative leader. The UN Charter of 1945, Article 1, gives the United Nations responsibility to 'maintain international peace and security' and over the years the UN has through numerous peace operations established itself as the leading peacebuilding agency.

Occasionally there might be a period where the UN forms a government alone, followed by a gradual or stepwise establishment of national authority, as in East Timor in 1999–2002. But this is so far the only example of the UN taking charge of the development of a new country from scratch.

The UN mandates

The UN peace operation mandates should of course be appropriate for the task. Unfortunately this is not always guaranteed. The Security Council's mandate for the UN Transitional Administration for East Timor (UNTAET), Resolution 1272 of October 1999, read:

- to provide security and maintain law and order throughout the territory of East Timor;
- to establish an effective administration;
- to assist in the development of civil and social services;
- to ensure the coordination and delivery of humanitarian assistance, rehabilitation and development assistance;
- to support capacity-building for self-government;
- to assist in the establishment of conditions for sustainable development.

This mandate did not give UNTAET the complete overall directive needed to build a state. The important aspect of economic development was not included; reconciliation was not mentioned and appeared only in a later UN mandate after the 2006 crisis.[9]

In general, the UN peacebuilding mandates do not cover all the essential aspects of peacebuilding. The wording of the mandates might also be non-specific, leaving much to interpretation. In East Timor, the UN was involved in conflict resolution and reconciliation, while the 1999 mandate for such activities would have to be found in the term 'establishment of conditions for sustainable development'.

We cannot assume that stronger and clearer mandates will ensure success. However, to the extent that mandates exist to guide us, they should be as adequate and relevant as possible. Reconciliation, which is often a missing component, should be a natural element from the start in most peace operations, whereas the mandate to support economic development is related to the issue of role-sharing and peacebuilding leadership.

One leader?

In East Timor, the World Bank came to play a leading role in economic development. This implied reconstruction and management of two major programmes, the Trust Fund for Timor Leste (TFET)[10] and the Transition Support Facility (TSP), as well as a yearly coordination meeting with the donor community. The UN government for its part addressed institutional development, security and to some extent reconciliation/conflict resolution. During the transition period the World Bank formally presented its plans to the UN for endorsement, but several researchers have observed rivalry between the two entities (for example, Merson *et al.*, 2006: 499).

While such a rivalry is clearly unfortunate, the main point here is that we should not have two masters. A complex challenge like peacebuilding needs strong and clear leadership. A government should normally be in charge, but whether it is or not, the international community should be represented by one overall peacebuilding leader. Economic development also represents an opportunity to boost reintegration, reconciliation and sound political development. Structured integration of economic development with other peacebuilding activities is therefore essential. The UN and the World Bank should find a better way to join forces but this would require a principled discussion that does not seem likely.

The need for peacebuilding skills

The quality of leadership is essential. Any SRSG (UN Special Representative of the Secretary General), resident coordinator or other person in charge should have broad knowledge of peacebuilding. The UN has made efforts to establish a pool of conflict experts available for mediation tasks at short notice. It seems a fact, however, that the leadership of long-term peacebuilding efforts is often left to career diplomats, who may or may not have a background in peacebuilding.

Lower-level leaders and other key personnel should also have peacebuilding skills based on experience, education/training or both. UN employment practices are complex, however, in that qualifications for the job are only one of several deciding factors. Others variables include nationality, gender, seniority and more.

Solli *et al.* (2011), studying recruitment of civilians for peacekeeping, pointed to the importance of personal contact and called for a 'significant overhaul of the UN recruitment system', observing that 'an increased number of trained personnel has not translated into higher deployment rates'.

If you happen to be appointed to a senior peacebuilding position without having the skills, let us hope for the sake of the country in question that you dare to raise the issue of training.

The 2006 UN architecture

In 2006 a new UN peacebuilding architecture was established, consisting of the Peacebuilding Commission, the Peacebuilding Fund and the Peacebuilding Support Office.

The Peacebuilding Commission (PBC) was created to provide strategic support, strengthen funding advocacy and coordination, and establish best practices. It consists of the Organisational Committee, a steering entity with representatives from 31 member countries, the Working Group on Lessons Learned and the Country Specific Configurations.

A country configuration, established for each country selected for support, comprises diplomats who visit at intervals. The PBC has, however, no operational mandate and is primarily an advisory entity.

The *Peacebuilding Support Office* (PBSO), headed by an Assistant Secretary General for Peacebuilding Support, was assigned to support the work of the Peacebuilding Commission and oversee the operation of the Peacebuilding Fund.

The *Peacebuilding Fund* (PBF) is a multi-donor trust fund that contributes to peacebuilding through allocations meant to meet early needs through the Immediate Response Facility and the Peacebuilding and Recovery Facility.

The *Immediate Response Facility* was created to address critical peacebuilding needs resulting from a conflict or dramatic change in a country. Project allocations are based on a strategic framework such as the UN Development Assistance Framework (UNDAF) (p. 135). These allocations are made by the PBF in New York.

The *Peacebuilding and Recovery Facility* involves programme-based financing, designed to address both critical and catalytic interventions, based inter alia on the priority plan for peacebuilding of the country concerned. Country allocations are handled by a joint steering committee, managed by the UN and the government of the actual country.

Has this new architecture strengthened the UN peacebuilding capacity? A full assessment is beyond the scope of this book. We may observe, however, that the PBC has brought increased support to the planning process. The PBF has also funded a variety of additional peacebuilding activities[11] and advocated for funding among donor countries while the PBC country configurations have helped identify implementing actors (see p. 137).

It seems clear that the PBC has done a good job in terms of fundraising advocacy. However, some writers are in doubt about its capacity for coordination. As discussed on pp. 134–135, one may also question the new architecture's approach to planning for peacebuilding.

As indicated above, the unfortunate one-year limit on national UN peace operations mandates does not pertain to the PBC, which is supposed to terminate its support in a given country only 'when foundations for sustainable peace and development are established' or subject to request by national authorities Security Council Resolution (1645: 5). We need to keep in mind, however, that the PBC's role is defined as advisory and not operational.

Working with the government

The UN's cooperation with a government may vary subject to the government's capacity and the territory's legal status. In the East Timor process, the UN formed a 'government' for a two-year transition period and then gradually reduced its involvement as the Timorese government's capacity grew. In Kosovo in 1999, the UN established a protectorate governing the area for seven years, while it still remained a part of Serbia.

In recent African operations the UN has made a point of underscoring that the government is in charge of the process and the UN's role is to provide support, even if the 2006 UN architecture is taking a more active role in peacebuilding planning.

Occasionally a local government may not want much help in managing the peacebuilding process. One such example is the Aceh peace process from 2005 onwards which benefited from the comprehensive financial support rendered to Indonesia after the tsunami in late 2004.

If the local government is in charge, it is imperative that the head of the government (president or prime minister) leads or gives strong support to the process. If the command is given to a minister or someone at a lower level, there may be a need to ensure that other ministers accept his/her leadership.

While the international community may have little influence in this regard, appropriate coordination among the international actors should be ensured. This is a natural UN task at a central level, while in the districts and in technical contexts other organisations may help out.

In East Timor, there was no overall coordination structure involving the many international organisations in the country.[12]

If you find such a situation when arriving in a mission, you should not feel shy about raising it with the UN leadership. If the SRSG is inaccessible, you might join forces with other organisations and agree on an initiative.

Regional and district authorities

Cooperation with the government must also include local authorities. Local administration should be part of overall peacebuilding plans, but even if there is no such plan, all contributing actors should look for opportunities to involve local government as peacebuilders. Constructive cooperation will help the local government to feel ownership and take responsibility.

One unfortunate aspect in some peacebuilding contexts is that the central government, perhaps representing the winners of a civil war, uses a democratic setting to centralise power and sideline existing local governance structures.

It is primarily the peacebuilding leadership's responsibility to relate to such challenges, but even if you work at a micro level out in the district, you should be aware of it and advocate cooperation and political dialogue whenever natural.

If local understanding of peacebuilding is missing, you may look for ways to create it.

A local mayor may be worried that peace is threatened by occasional outbreaks of violence in an area where you work. Can she be invited to discuss the sources of violence and possible cooperation on reconciliation efforts? Would a presentation and discussion of other peacebuilding topics be of interest?

Partnerships of various kinds between local government and international or local organisations may be possible. For example, providing health services is a government task but may in times of need be managed/supported by local and international organisations with a view to local empowerment.

Any support activity may offer opportunities of constructive dialogue on peacebuilding and cooperation.

Working with other local actors

If there is no local government in charge, are there other local actors you can work with? With support, can the parties to a conflict get involved? (Antagonism could make this difficult.) Can local civilian organisations play a role, such as being focal points for sector cooperation, dialogue and seminars? Do any of the organisations have a wide network and command the respect of the parties to the conflict?

If the government is actively involved, could a civilian organisation become the government's partner and link with other organisations? Could religious organisations get together for a joint peace effort? If no one is capable, is empowerment the answer? Is it perhaps a matter of training, equipment and proper office facilities? Local organisations sometimes have excellent manpower but lack the means needed.

In Northern Ireland the Community Relations Council assumed the task of establishing connections between peacebuilding activities and providing an inventory of peace-related activities (Lederach, 1997).

In Sierra Leone the National Red Cross Society, supported by the International Federation of Red Cross/Red Crescent Societies,[13] trained a large number of civilians and established a network of 48 local committees that served as focal points for:

- conflict analysis and peacebuilding activities
- rebuilding families
- reintegration of ex-combatants
- sport and cultural events
- local organisations.

A gradual transition

Local actors should get involved and learn to take responsibility for as much as possible of the peacebuilding process as early as possible. This can be a difficult balance. A war-torn country may be sapped of human resources, while at the same time its future should be defined by its own people. The international community is often accused of handling this poorly. 'To get things done' it may be tempting to disregard local actors.

Do not be surprised if you find that you have to remind your colleagues (or even yourself) of the need to involve local partners. The general norm must be: involve local actors in planning and implementation to the extent that their capacity allows as early as possible at all levels. Make plans for capacity development if you can. To the extent that you have the authority, you should aim to transfer it in a structured manner while providing the support needed throughout the process. This is no easy task, but the point here is to be conscious about it from day one.

Needs analysis

To address challenges, we need to know them. As observed above, peacebuilding is about addressing interests, some of which are basic human needs and therefore essential. For our purpose here we use the term 'needs analysis'.

How do we identify interests/needs and decide what action is required? A simple approach is to start out with two macro questions:

- What will this country look like when lasting peace is secured? If we are clear on how it should look versus how it looks today, we have identified the needs.
- What must we do to get there? That is, what measures does it take to meet the needs?

These are of course not mathematical questions. It is never possible to establish exactly what it takes to establish peace. But if we do not try to answer these questions, we are more likely to start out with limited ideas of the needs and unclear concepts of what action is required.

If we just start 'building peace' without having an adequate picture of the needs, our efforts may in the worst case end up being destructive.

The needs in question will be diverse, related to security, welfare, justice and reconciliation, to different aspects of a functioning state, to systemic challenges, culture and more. Diverse and complex, these needs are often hard to detect and intricately interwoven.

What kind of analysis is needed?

When we try to build peace in a country, we relate to social, historical, cultural, economic, demographic, sociological, psychological, legal and political aspects. All of these aspects might hold information that is essential to peace, and due analysis should therefore include them all.

It seems a fair assumption that the frequent relapses into violence during the first five years of peacebuilding processes[14] has to do with the lack of such analyses. (As we shall see, East Timor is one such example.)

Each sector of public administration requires analysis of status and needs, as do governance, the judiciary and security. A thorough conflict analysis (discussed below) is a crucial component, unless it is done as a separate exercise.

The overall purpose of the analysis is to define what appears needed to ensure peace. Such a comprehensive task requires expertise in fields like social anthropology, sociology, political science, economy, law and social psychology, as well as thorough knowledge of the country's history, culture and traditions.

An extensive analysis takes time, and will necessarily imply considerable field and desk research. Interviews are needed with politicians, traditional and religious leaders, representatives of various interest groups, such as war veterans, women and youth, and other stakeholders at all levels of society. (On possible use of IT and GIS Technology, see p. 140).

How long would this take? As it has probably never been done, there is no experience to substantiate an estimate, but several months would surely be required to provide what is necessary. In the meantime urgent activities should go ahead. It may also be possible to do a level-based approach, like the one the Swedish aid agency SIDA suggests for conflict analysis (p. 113). This means starting with an overall strategic analysis before moving on to sector and regional/local analyses.

The focus of the analysis must necessarily be on the interests and needs of today, as people's situation changes in conflict settings. Any analysis used as a basis for peacebuilding planning must therefore be fresh and updated at intervals.

The need for conflict analysis

This is arguably the most important element in the preplanning analysis. 'Sketchy understanding of a conflict and unchecked assumptions can produce interventions that actually worsen tensions and fuel the conflicts they seek to mitigate' (OECD/DAC, 2007: 7).

Since conflicts are the reason why peacebuilding is needed in the first place, one might expect the UN to make conflict resolution and reconciliation a priority, and therefore take the steps needed to understand all relevant aspects of a conflict. Unfortunately this has rarely been the case, and again, the East Timor operations offer a striking illustration.

From the beginning of its operations in 1999 to when the crisis erupted in 2006, the UN did not conduct any comprehensive conflict analysis. The UN missions did submit internal situational and routine analytical reports, but nothing that could provide the profound understanding needed. One of the main factors behind the crisis in 2006, an east/west rift in the population, was largely unknown to both the UN and the international community as a whole, even if it reflected an antagonism that had existed since early colonial times. A comprehensive conflict analysis might have revealed these crucial facts and given the UN a chance to relate to the issue early on (Ofstad, 2012).

A proper conflict analysis includes mapping of existing conflicts, parties and stakeholders, identification of the drivers of the conflicts and the threats they represent, the potential for new or changing conflicts,[15] and the needs and possibilities of conflict resolution/mitigation and reconciliation.[16] The analysis must also take into account the likely effects of the peacebuilding process as well as other trends and developments in society.

A conflict analysis may be a separate effort or included in an overall needs analysis. More importantly, one needs the same multidisciplinary approach as outlined for the overall needs analysis, and the same range of expertise.

Over the years, a number of conflict-related analyses of the East Timor situation were conducted by researchers with different academic backgrounds. Some offer incisive studies of the conflict dynamics, others present important social, ethnic, historical and demographic factors. None of them are sufficient if seen in isolation and most of them came too late, but put together they constitute a much more enlightening picture.

If a highly qualified multidisciplinary team had conducted a comprehensive joint analysis early on, the East Timor peacebuilding leadership might have had a powerful planning and conflict management tool at hand.

Who should do it?

In recent years, the international community's interest in conflict analysis has increased, and many actors have developed analytical capacity. For instance, South Sudan has been the subject of a variety of analyses. The World Bank developed its own Conflict Analysis Framework (CAF) in 2005 and has shared reports with host governments.[17] The comprehensive, multidisciplinary approach suggested here is generally not applied, however, and many analyses are primarily meant to support one actor's activities.

Given its responsibility to support peacebuilding processes, should we expect the UN to provide governments with the analyses needed? The UN does at times conduct internal conflict analysis, in so-called TAMs (Technical Assessment Missions), conducted by the Department for Peacekeeping Operations, and SAMs (Strategic Assessment Missions), led by the UN Department of Political Affairs. However, these documents are not the comprehensive multidisciplinary analysis suggested above. Neither are they shared with the government in charge, and therefore they are of limited value to the planning process.

In 2004, the *Interagency Framework on Conflict Analysis in Transition Situations*, developed by the UN Development Group (UNDG) and the UN Executive Committee on Humanitarian Affairs (ECHA), suggested that 'a transitional strategy of the UN for countries emerging from violent conflict should be based upon a standardised inter-agency methodology for conflict analysis' (UNDG/ECHA, 2004: 1), and, importantly, that it should feed into UN planning frameworks as well as 'into national development plans' (p. 14). The document even contains advice on how to advocate for government involvement in the analysis process.

Christopher Wilson's report *Overcoming Violent Conflict. Peace and Development (DPA) in Indonesia* (2005) is an example of a comprehensive conflict analysis facilitated by the UN. A team of 10 academics, many of them PhD students with a conflict research background, plus local staff were engaged to study three Indonesian regions. The inclusive UNDG/ECHA analysis framework of 2004 was not applied, as it was completed only after the work had started. Still, the analysis was termed a cooperation effort with the government. It drew on consultative local workshops and inputs from public institutions, including the State Ministry of National Planning.[18] Although this nearly one-year-long process concluded with mostly generic recommendations that may not have been used by the Indonesian government, it was an indication of the capacity the UN may be able to provide.

In 2006, the establishment of the UN Peacebuilding Commission (p. 105), with the mandate of providing strategic peacebuilding support, gave reason to expect increased UN support/involvement in conflict-related needs analysis.

Instead the UN's approach in several later peacebuilding operations in Africa has been to look to the government for the identification of needs. Examples are found in Burundi, Sierra Leone, Guinea-Bissau and the Central African Republic (CAR). The UN's level of involvement appears to have differed, but in Burundi and the CAR the UN asked the governments to develop priority plans for peacebuilding, to identify prime peacebuilding needs.[19] These priority plans would serve as a basis for further planning and for allocations from the Peacebuilding Fund, a standard approach for countries selected for support.

The UN practice of asking the government to spell out peacebuilding priorities, instead of offering help to provide the analysis needed, may have to do with increasing international emphasis on local ownership. China and India have expressed concerns about the UN imposing its peacebuilding ideas on developing countries (Gheciu and Welsh, 2009). The Fourth High Level Forum on Aid Effectiveness in 2011 highlighted the need for national ownership, and the G7+ advocates a model of post-conflict transition where 'countries assess their own situation, using tools that they have developed'.[20]

The problem is, however, that governments of countries in need of peacebuilding are part of the conflict equation. They may represent the winners of the war and are often accused of gross partisan behaviour, meaning they are hardly in an ideal position to provide the analysis needed. Another concern is war-torn countries' capacity for such tasks.

This given, how can the government and/or the peacebuilding leadership get the analysis needed? If we consider it a UN responsibility to support the government but also acknowledge the need for local ownership, is the example from Indonesia something to build on? Can we envision a multidisciplinary team of seasoned experts being offered to the government, not to carry out a UN mission but to work with and for the government?

Indigenous expertise would have to be involved, while international experts would add to the perspective. If we consider the amount of expertise found world-wide among academic institutions, think-tanks and practitioners, such human resources would surely be available. A condition must be that the team would work with total integrity and present its own perception of the truth, something all governments might not want. But, if accepted, such an approach could provide an improved basis for peacebuilding and development planning. And one might hope that this kind of external assistance would not be considered an imposition.

A level-based approach?

As observed above, proper analysis takes time, and peacebuilding and development planning should take place early on. A possible approach might be a level-based analysis. SIDA's *Manual for Conflict Analysis* (2006) suggests a minimum of six to 12 weeks for a strategic conflict analysis. Next, subject to the equation, one may move on to sector-based or regional and local analysis, which might then feed into ongoing planning processes or be used for adjustments.

Meanwhile, the peacebuilding process would have to start. That is, operation mandates would be defined, the mission established, and urgent needs like security addressed.

Your own analysis?

You may find that there is no adequate conflict analysis that covers your geographical area or the conflict aspects you relate to in your work. If so, could your organisation provide what is necessary? If we are talking about a profound analysis, this is a comprehensive and expensive task. Is it an option for you to do an analysis yourself?

If there are other colleagues/organisations with a similar need, could you initiate a conflict analysis workshop? As far as possible, your agency and its partners should in any case base their activities on a shared perception of the conflict landscape.

If you choose to hold a workshop, you should consider inviting resource persons from the local community. But how do you do the analysis?

You will find that that this issue is closely linked to both the Conflict Impact Assessment (p. 147) and the 'do no harm' concept (p. 148).

There is a variety of models available.[21] Prominent examples are:

Vaux, Goodhand and Walker (2002) *Conducting Conflict Assessments: Guidance Notes*, DFID;

UNDG/ECHA (2004) *Interagency Framework for Conflict Analysis in Transition situations*;

SIDA (2006) *Manual for Conflict Analysis*.

While these analysis frameworks might be too complex and demanding for an ad hoc workshop in the field, the following approach includes suggestions from all of them, but in a simpler package.

The purpose

Start out by identifying the purpose of the analysis. Is it to get the best possible understanding of the conflict landscape, including all relevant aspects? If so, you may wish to map and discuss international aspects as well as national and local ones, even if you are working in a far-flung village. However, if the most important issue is how to relate to conflicts in your own working equation, prime questions would be:

- How may the conflicts affect your activities and results?
- How may your activities affect the conflicts, negatively and positively?
- What you can do to prevent negative influences and create or increase positive ones?

So how do you address these questions?

Actor analysis

To establish the clearest possible picture of the conflict actors, the following questions should be addressed:

- Who are the parties to the conflicts?
- What are their positions and attitudes?
- What are their interests, including hidden ones?
- Who is affected by the conflicts, and what are their interests?
- Who may influence the conflicts?
- Are there linkages between the actors? If so, what do they imply, positively and negatively?
- What are the actors' capacities for doing harm?
- What are the actors' capacities for positive change?

Analysis of key conflict factors

You should have the best possible understanding of the conflict dynamics. This is about mapping and understanding underlying factors, asking:

- What are the causes of the conflicts?
- What are the conflict drivers today?
- What could be future drivers, given expected developments?

These factors could be about:

- political/governance and legal aspects;
- economic aspects;
- social, including historical, ethnographic, demographic, cultural, psychological and religious aspects, etc.

Without expertise and comprehensive studies, we should normally not expect to gain profound understanding of a complex conflict landscape. Still, a workshop drawing on the knowledge of all participants may bring insights that benefit them all.

Try to establish the likely development of the conflicts in case there is no intervention or external influence. Are they going to affect the security of the community and the organisations involved?

You should try to map possible conflict triggers, meaning more immediate factors that may lead to the outbreak of violence or escalation. Examples are crime, human rights abuse, election fraud, public rallies, etc.

Practical consequences

Once you have achieved a fair understanding of the conflicts, their actors, triggers, dynamics and security aspects, you may also wish to agree on adequate action. To this end, the topics presented in the 'Do no harm' section (p. 148) should be discussed. This would be about:

1 How to avoid the conflicts influencing your activities negatively.
   Examples: How can you avoid warlords stealing provisions? How can you withstand pressure to favour strong groups of beneficiaries? Do you need to take security precautions?
2 How to avoid your activities causing negative effects.
   Examples: How do you avoid contributing to a war economy? How do you avoid sustaining fault-lines? How do you avoid rivalry over distribution?
3 How to contribute to reconciliation or conflict resolution.
   Examples: Can you utilise or create connectors (see pp. 145 and 151)? Can you suggest/encourage partnerships? Can you initiate cooperation between adversaries (see p. 128)? Can you contribute to a peace economy?

Make sure someone writes a report from the workshop, reflecting all important findings and conclusions.

An analytical challenge to keep in mind relates to how we expect the country or area to develop. Will there be a transitional national unity government? Will there be a party-based democracy or a model based on a council of elders? Will there be a liberal market open to free trade, and who will get a peace dividend, if any? Such factors, which relate to our discussions of 'What kind of peace?' (pp. 30–31), are likely to influence the conflict landscape. While the government may offer answers to these questions, there will always be uncertainties, reminding us that such analyses can never be entirely accurate, and that all we can do is our best.

In general we need to remember that conflict landscapes change with time, sometimes fast. Some conflicts may be resolved, while new ones emerge and alliances change. Keeping abreast of developments will therefore require you to update the analysis after some time.

Common needs

Let us, despite common practice, assume that the analyses needed have been carried out. What kind of needs should we expect to deal with? Let us look at some of the most frequently addressed needs of a dysfunctional society, before devoting special focus to the often ignored need for conflict resolution/reconciliation. On pp. 130–132 you will find a summary of both kinds included in a 'needs menu'.

Security and civil rights

Security is an urgent need in most peace operations. In the aftermath of violence there is always a risk of flare-ups because of hatred, rivalries, unsettled scores or crime. To prevent physical attacks, there is normally a need for credible security forces. These should ideally be local police or military, although UN peacekeeping forces and UN police are often required. In addition to addressing acute protection needs, UN security personnel may encounter challenges in training local police, who might be unqualified or dysfunctional after the war. Indeed, local police may sometimes be carriers of violent traditions themselves.

There is normally also scope for civilian contributions to security. The UNHCR often does a comprehensive job in protecting exposed groups and individuals (see Chapter 5), as does the ICRC. Without resources other than their organisation's name and ethical clout, such civilian actors can mean the difference between life and death to many.

A young male refugee from Bosnia, who planned to return home after the war in 1996, narrated his story on a 'go and see trip', arranged by the UNHCR and the International Organisation for Migration:

> I was in a concentration camp in Banja Luka. We were tortured and got only one bread each, every second week. We were certain we were going to die. But then the International Red Cross Committee managed to get access to the camp, and from that moment on things started improving. We got more food, the torture declined and after some time UNHCR was able to take us out and bring us to other countries.'[22]

Other civilian actors such as Amnesty International and the International Crisis Group may contribute by reporting on human rights abuses, which are often rife in the wake of a war.

In addition to physical protection, people need access to a functioning judiciary, for example to get their home back from an illegal occupier, compensation for harm sustained and a variety of rights that need fulfilment to stabilise society. However, subject to resource availability and the status of the country's judiciary before the war, making the judiciary effective and responsible may take a long time.

Disarmament and demobilisation

These are often pressing needs. Disarmament may take place as part of demobilisation after a peace agreement or in an effort to scale down armed forces. It may be about disempowering militant groups or armed gangs, including freedom fighters, criminals or civilians who keep arms for self-protection. Civilian delegates should not be directly involved in the practical side of disarmament, which is a military task. However, on a political level the international community may try to contain the parties' access to arms, as disarmament may otherwise be futile. Sometimes disarmament necessitates action against the trade in drugs, diamonds and other illicit goods. If you happen to hold a senior UN position, you might need to discuss such needs with the government or peacekeeping forces.

Even peaceful civilians will not give up their weapons easily if they feel their security is threatened. It may be difficult to assess whether civilians should be allowed to keep arms for security or other purposes. And there is a risk that good efforts may turn bad in heated conflict situations. Such disarmament demands a thorough risk assessment, and should be part of a comprehensive approach to restoring security. Attacks on disarmed civilians may destroy people's trust in the peacebuilding process. The point to observe is that when disarming civilians, one must also remove their need to possess arms.

Post-violence periods may offer rich possibilities for criminal elements. Disarmament of criminal individuals or gangs may be a precondition for safe peacebuilding. If you interact with the government or peacekeeping forces, you might need to raise this issue.

There may be numerous armed groups in a post-violence environment. Even if we assume that there is full commitment to peace from all armed groups, their interests and situation must be taken into account. Their role as combatants may be a part of their identity. After a long war they may have no other skills apart from fighting. Giving up their arms, meaning the tools of their trade, therefore constitutes a heavy demand. The weapons may also represent economic value, and the combatant's future may be uncertain.

Rewards are frequently used to meet these concerns. The combatant may be given a sum of money, agricultural equipment, food, construction materials or other benefits. The use of rewards can, however, be problematic for war victims, who may have been subjected to atrocities by the beneficiaries. The best way to handle this issue may be to give the reward to the combatants' community. This lessens the impression that a reward is going to an individual, at the same time providing an entrance ticket back to civilian life for the fighter, who may have become estranged from his own community.

While civilian actors will normally not play an active role in demobilisation, they could be requested to help out with a pre-assessment of the soldiers' needs and perhaps transport to their home area. While there is nothing wrong with such involvement, the risk of being associated with armed forces must be borne in mind (see p. 32).[23]

Reintegration of former combatants

Successful reintegration of ex-combatants can be crucial for the restoration of peace. The former fighters need to return to a normal family life, to resume civilian vocations and to re-establish sound relationships with civil society. This can be a long and painful process, sometimes requiring long-term support to the ex-combatants, who might otherwise easily get involved in crime or violent political activities. Support programmes may include allocation of land, agricultural support, job placement, credit schemes, etc. The combatant's family may be given psychosocial support, counselling and perhaps school fees for children.

The process might involve a number of organisations and public entities. Peacebuilders need to ensure that the reintegration issue is addressed and well planned before organised disarmament takes place.

The community might, as mentioned above, be the recipient of the combatant's disarmament reward. The support programme should therefore be developed in close interaction with the communities involved. While it is important to ensure that the combatants successfully adapt to normal life, there might be other people in the community who are worse off and reintegration incentives should not foster envy and conflict. Inviting local society to play an active role in the process may help to prevent such negative effects. Sometimes community processes may even involve spiritual and ritualistic approaches.

> The specificity of the mato oput ceremonies in northern Uganda and of the efforts to reintegrate former child soldiers in Sierra Leone is the use of ritualistic ingredients – stepping on an egg, washing away the evil past with holy water or oil, drinking the juice of a plant or a tree, evoking ancestors, provoking trance. Spirits dominate the scenario in Mozambique.
>
> (Huyse, 2008)

Mine clearance

Numerous attempts have been made to ban anti-personnel mines. One of them led to the Ottawa Mine Ban Treaty, signed and brought into force in 1999. The treaty has had positive effects on limiting the trade in mines. Thirty-eight nations stopped producing them and all signatories committed themselves not to sell anti-personnel mines to other countries. There are, however, still a number of manufacturing nations, among which the US, Russia and China are the most prominent. There are also enormous stockpiles in a large number of countries. The curse of these weapons will therefore remain a factor in violent conflicts for the foreseeable future. Mine clearance programmes should consist of:

- a technical aspect which is about detecting, marking, removing or destroying mines;
- a social/economic component which includes human development.

Practical approaches have been developed in the Bad Honnef Guidelines, adopted by United Mine Action Services, UNICEF and a number of other organisations. Military agencies as well as humanitarian organisations carry out mine clearance.

If your organisation is taking on this challenge, coordination with military actors may be a prime task.

Institution building

Institution building is often a core task in the stabilisation and development of peace.

As we have seen in East Timor, there might at times be a need to build a state with all the required governance and management institutions from scratch. This implies a heavy responsibility, not only because it must be done properly but also because values and principles are reflected in institution building. Do we initiate a human rights institution? What kind of training do we provide for judges and police officers?

Even if there is a government, the international community may exert a lot of influence as to which institutions are built and how. Our responsibility here is related to the discussion of what kind of peace we wish to support (pp. 30–31). We should also be aware of the issue of sovereignty, which must be treated delicately if we are to progress effectively (see Zaum, 2007). General requirements are to take local stakeholders seriously, engage them in discussions, and try to help them find solutions they can acknowledge as their own.

The UN is a key actor in institution building, and has in some instances proved quite effective. In East Timor, within two years, the UN helped the Timorese establish democratic institutions, a local government with a functioning central administration, a police force and an army. UN experts worked with Timorese counterparts to ensure transfer of knowledge, drawing on whatever human resources were available after the brain drain of the war. Not all efforts were successful, but the achievements were considerable.

Economic development

War generally means a dramatic economic setback, necessitating revival and development. Major actors like the International Monetary Fund (IMF) and the World Bank group, including the International Bank for Reconstruction and Development, supported by regional development banks, often play an important role. Efforts at the macro level may include economic reforms, technical support to the government's finance administration and strengthening/development of a national central bank. Inter-communal trade, exports and the promotion of private investment may also be included. Economic support might be subject to regulatory and practical reform by the government to ensure that the desired level of cooperation and progress is achieved.

At the micro level, international organisations may contribute in various ways, such as community development programmes, small-scale saving/credit programmes, infrastructure improvement, agricultural projects, vocational education, and more.

The international community has at times been accused of importing western capitalism, in disregard of local traditions and interests. (This relates to the discussion of 'What kind of peace?', pp. 30–31). While a profound analysis of this topic is beyond the scope of this book, we should always keep in mind the need to respect indigenous interests and to uphold the right to self-determination. The needs analysis suggested above would go some way to facilitate cooperation with local actors. And if such analysis is missing, there should at least be a profound dialogue on economic direction and the establishment of priorities with the country's government and other stakeholders.

As suggested above (pp. 104–105), all peacebuilding activities including economic development should ideally be integrated under one leadership. However, the Bretton Woods institutions (the IMF and the World Bank system) can hardly be expected to give up their independent role.

Job creation

In a citizen survey conducted for the 2011 *World Development Report*, unemployment was characterised as 'overwhelmingly the most important factor cited for recruitment into gangs and rebel movements' (World Bank, 2011).

After a war we typically find many unemployed youth in the community, many of them combat-trained, with no prospect of an income. This is a dangerous situation and, as observed under 'Urgent issues' (pp. 98–99), it should be an early priority to get these idle youths off the streets and into gainful activities. However, substantial resources are needed to employ large numbers of people, and this problem is hardly ever adequately tackled.

To compound the challenge, potential large-scale employment schemes have to be time-limited, which means that needs are likely to re-emerge at the end of a scheme. Still, the suggestion here, in line with the 2011 *World Development Report*, is that the international community should give this need higher priority. If initial large employment schemes are combined with efforts aiming at more sustainable employment, for instance through vocational training, establishment of small credit banking, etc., the stability achieved during the most critical period might be of long-term value.

Sound political development

Article 21 of the Universal Declaration of Human Rights reads:

1. Everyone has the right to take part in the government of his country, directly or through freely chosen representatives.
2. Everyone has the right to equal access to public service in his country.
3. The will of the people shall be the basis of the authority of government; this shall be expressed in periodic and genuine elections which shall be by universal and equal suffrage and shall be held in secret vote or by equivalent free voting procedures.

Support for the development of democracy is widely considered a cornerstone in peacebuilding. Democratic states are generally regarded as more successful than totalitarian ones. There is a broad consensus that internal conflicts are easier to resolve in democracies, and that democracies do not easily wage wars against each other.

The benefits of a well-functioning democracy are not disputed here. However, as observed in 'What kind of peace?' (pp. 30–31), democratic reform must, like any other development, take place on the terms of the recipient country. Anything imposed will unavoidably lead to negative reactions and is unlikely to succeed (remember Brehm's reactance theory discussed on p. 88).

Questions we should raise at an early stage with the people and political stakeholders in any given peacebuilding situation are:

- How would you like your country to be governed, centrally and locally? If there is little democratic experience in the country, there may be a need to invest in training/discussions of what democratic models imply.
- What role should traditional governance structures and practices play? A new system that clashes with local traditions may come as an unpleasant surprise and in the long run undermine peace. (See the below example of East Timor.)
- Is a cabinet based on simple parliamentary majority right for you at this stage, or would a national unity government be preferable? Developing a sense of national unity may be crucial for a war-torn country's peace and stability.
- Is the society ready for elections? If a society is still divided by profound conflicts, democratic elections may imply war by other means. Should preliminary arrangements be considered for an agreed transition period?
- Should any particular groups or interests be ensured representation in parliament? This could be about ethnicity, women and under-privileged groups.

Such questions should be part of a national process of discussion/analysis. While young democracies need cooperation and dialogue on peaceful development, they are frequently plagued by a winner takes all attitude. Governments may use all available means to ensure their own power, including employing their supporters in all positions that count, using a simple majority to push through anything that serves their interests, effectively sidelining the opposition and making dialogue and cooperation impossible.

Sidelined groups and individuals, who dreamt of freedom and joint nation-building, may find such exclusion hard to live with.

In East Timor, introduction of party-based local elections clashed with the existing community governance system of elders elected on merit. If the elders joined political parties, they risked losing the independence and some of the integrity that had previously earned them respect.

Even comprehensive dialogue does not necessarily guarantee a sustainable outcome. A dialogue project in the CAR, supported by the UN, involved numerous political actors and militia factions in a lengthy process that eventually led to the 2009 establishment of a national unity government. Unfortunately, the president was later accused of sidelining ministers outside his own party, and some of them left the government.

While there is no guarantee of success, the least we can do is to give dialogue our best efforts. While the CAR project may have failed due to political self-interest, it does represent the kind of effort we need to explore.

Electoral assistance

Subject to the outcome of the dialogue process, the international community may be asked to support and monitor elections. While this is a big task in itself, it may also necessitate a census to ensure a controlled process. In some cases, such as Afghanistan in 2001, a preliminary constitution may also provide a roadmap towards proper establishment of a country's final constitution.

Before a monitoring mission there is normally an assessment mission to verify the need for monitoring, to assess security and to ensure that the observation is likely to work. Ideally, the monitoring of elections should encompass the election campaign and voter registration, as well as the election itself and post-election parliamentary development. Unfortunately, it is often limited to the election.

Election observers should have a good understanding of the electoral law of the country concerned and, if possible, some experience of election monitoring. They should be trained and have a joint briefing before the mission starts to ensure that their reports are standardised and that they all interpret questionnaires and relevant information in the same way. The international community has a long way to go in developing good monitoring practices. There is a general need to shift the focus from short-term monitoring missions to more thorough, longer-term efforts (Van der Weyden, 'Election monitoring', in Reychler and Paffenholz, 2001).

Social services

Some services may be crucial to stability. Economic decline is usually accompanied by a rise in poverty, and assistance to vulnerable people is often badly needed. While immediate needs for food, shelter and medical services might be addressed by external organisations such as the UN World Food Programme, UNICEF, the Red Cross/Red Cresent, Médecins sans Frontières, Oxfam, Save the Children and others, the promotion of self-help should be addressed as early as possible. Helping large numbers of people with food and shelter is not feasible for a poor state, but a functioning agriculture ministry might provide active advice and help people start revival programmes.

The need for conflict resolution and reconciliation

As observed above, the conflict landscape may be very complex. As peacebuilders, we should aim to address all conflicts that could represent a threat to peace. For our discussion here we again assume the unlikely scenario that a proper conflict analysis has been conducted or updated, providing us with the understanding we need. That is, we know the needs for conflict resolution and reconciliation.

Relevant mediation approaches and techniques are presented in Chapter 4. But we should also try to ensure that people have access to conflict resolution mechanisms of their own. Moreover, there will often be deep-seated hatred, suspicion and wounds that cannot be addressed through mediation. This is primarily about the need for reconciliation, which may be addressed through a variety of measures, often disregarded in peacebuilding operations.

Resolution mechanisms

A functioning judiciary may be crucial to peace. Sometimes there will be other local mechanisms in place, such as councils of elders or village leaders acting as courts or mediators. Entities offering arbitration may supplement the courts. Reviving or supporting such mechanisms can be essential.

Subject to their standing in the local community, international organisations may sometimes help establish new institutions that gain the community's respect. The community councils in Sierra Leone (p. 108) provide one such example, another is the institution of Ombudsman established in Bosnia after the war in 1996. As a general rule one should always explore existing or traditional resolution mechanisms and their potential before suggesting new ones.

The UN and reconciliation

'Largely missing from peacebuilding work so far in South Sudan has been attention to broad-based reconciliation and the legacies of decades of South–South conflict on ordinary citizen' (Reeve, 2012).

Addressing reconciliation needs is a natural peacebuilding task. However, analysis of the UN's major peacebuilding operations shows that this element often receives perfunctory attention. While the UN might do a great job in institution building, provision of security and to some extent economic development, while also addressing issues of dialogue/conflict resolution, the need for large-scale reconciliation is rarely adequately addressed.

Truth and reconciliation commissions are frequently on the peacebuilding agenda at an early stage, but realisation is often problematic, and their outreach may be limited.

In East Timor, the Commission for Reception, Truth and Reconciliation (CAVR), which was established with UN support in 2002, handled only a limited number of the cases it considered 'eligible'. The CAVR's proposal of 2005 to establish a country-wide community-based reconciliation programme (CAVR, 2005) had not been realised as of January 2014.

Both Burundi and the Central African Republic had proposals for truth and reconciliation commissions included in the strategic frameworks that the UN helped them develop in 2007 and 2008 respectively (Ofstad, 2012). However, the CAR had not established such a commission before the government was overthrown in a coup in March 2013, and Burundi still had no commission as of January 2014.

It should be noted that the UN mandates concerning reconciliation are typically worded in terms of supporting indigenous activities, as opposed to defining an active role for the UN. This fact may be connected to the concern of big international actors such as China and India about the UN imposing its ideas on developing countries (see Gheciu and Welsh, 2009).

Given the lack of indigenous capacity in war-torn countries, the UN's lack of involvement in reconciliation may be one of the reasons why a majority of the population never get the help required to reconcile, even if they desire it.

Would a friendly offer from the UN to help a government with implementation of reconciliation programmes be considered an imposition? We may not get to know the answer anytime soon as there is no indication that the UN is planning to become more directly involved.

To the extent that the UN supports the establishment of truth and reconciliation commissions, it generally suggests a link to transitional justice, which means that serious criminal cases revealed through the reconciliation process will be prosecuted.

In Burundi, the plans for a Truth and Reconciliation Commission may have been stalled by a disagreement between the UN and the government on issues of prosecution and impunity (Security Council Report S/2013/36; Ofstad, 2012). Because of governments' interest in avoiding prosecution, they often take a reluctant stand on transitional justice.[24]

Is the UN approach appropriate? Reconciliation does not necessarily need to be linked to prosecution. It is possible to undertake a reconciliation process regardless of crime, which could be prosecuted even if the perpetrator and the victim are reconciled. If so, it will be for the prosecution and the courts to assess whether efforts to reconcile should influence the punishment.

Prosecution or amnesty?

While reconciliation does not exclude justice, amnesty does. This is one of the most difficult questions in peacebuilding. To what extent should crimes committed during a violent conflict be punished? Some societies have opted for full amnesty, others for prosecution, at least for serious offences. The problem typically occurs during a phase of change, where a fragile new democracy is being established after a period of oppression and violence.

The main arguments for prosecution are:

1 Prosecution is a moral obligation towards the victims of crime.
2 It is a cleansing process for society.
3 It gives the new regime moral authority, and mistrust and cynicism may be avoided.
4 Criminals can be removed from the scene to prevent corruption of the new regime.
5 Prosecution is a deterrent against future human rights abuse.

The counter-arguments are:

1 Justice administered by the winners cannot be fair.
2 Prosecutions may destabilise a new and fragile regime.
3 Purging a large number of civil servants and officers may weaken a new regime.
4 Legal principles may be disregarded, typically:
   - the principle that penal sanctions should be based on existing law, given that post-violence phase regimes sometimes introduce new laws to pursue old crimes;
   - statutes of limitation, whereby prosecution must take place within a specified period after the crime, may be changed or violated.
5 Prosecution is counterproductive to reconciliation.

There is clearly no general solution to this problem. A strong state may be able to afford to apply a high level of accountability whereas a fragile one may have to tread more carefully. The sentiments and moral norms of the affected population must be considered as well as the risk of renewed violence by groups who feel threatened by justice. The majority of post-violence regimes seem to choose leniency as the guiding principle, a choice possibly influenced by the desire to protect their own supporters. Among more than 100 internal armed conflicts in the period 1982–1996, only 40 were followed by prosecution (Huyse, 'Amnesty, Truth or prosecution', in Reychler and Paffenholz, 2001).

Most writers are in agreement that crimes against humanity should always be pursued, and that society must otherwise try to strike a balance between prosecution and reconciliation.

National reconciliation efforts

Truth and reconciliation commissions

What characterises the process of truth and reconciliation? According to Hikias Asefa, who played an active role in the South African reconciliation process, the following elements are essential (Asefa in Reychler and Paffenholz, 2001: 340):

- Honest acknowledgement of the harm or injury each party has inflicted on the other.
- Sincere regret and remorse for the injury done.
- Readiness to apologise for one's role in inflicting the injury.
- Readiness of the conflicting parties to let go of the anger and the bitterness caused by the conflict and the injury.
- Commitment by the offender not to repeat the injury.

- Sincere effort to redress past grievances that caused the conflict and to compensate for the damage caused to the extent possible.
- Entering into a new mutually enriching relationship.

How can conflicting parties possibly achieve all this? As in mediation, there would be a facilitator to help structure the dialogue. However, as opposed to mediation, the parties presenting their cases are allowed to try to establish why the adversary is responsible. The purpose here is to make the adversary admit guilt, change future behaviour and make amends.

The parties frequently blame their own acts on their adversaries: 'I did what I did because of your behaviour.' It is the task of the facilitator to help the parties see their own role and admit guilt to the extent relevant. This is clearly challenging given the general human reluctance to admit mistakes and the emotional barriers that must be overcome. Still, some truth and reconciliation commissions have made significant achievements. Some well-known cases are:

- the Chilean National Commission on Truth and Reconciliation (1990);
- the International Truth Commission in El Salvador (1991);
- the South African Truth and Reconciliation Commission (1995–1998);
- the Rwanda National Unity and Reconciliation Commission (1998).

Other approaches to national reconciliation?

While truth and reconciliation commissions may be effective in addressing wounds related to crime and offences, their capacity for large-scale outreach to the people is normally limited.

East Timor's CAVR observed in its report of November 2005 that in total, 1,113 cases had been processed, less than one-quarter of the cases it considered 'eligible', and that a new independent entity for broad-scale reconciliation in the communities should be established. Referring to a grassroots demand, the commission observed that there was a continuous need for people to come to terms with what had happened, and a national, community-based programme was required to address these needs. Unfortunately, the CAVR report received quite a measured response from East Timor's president, and, as observed above, the proposal had not been implemented by January 2014.

The idea of a national community-focused reconciliation entity, which clearly deserved a much better destiny, is worth considering wherever there are large-scale reconciliation needs.

National reconciliation is a term frequently used in both governmental and UN documents, but its substance is normally limited. Comprehensive nation-wide efforts, such as the one suggested for East Timor, may never have been applied anywhere.

Dialogue is an essential element in reconciliation and at times the UN has supported important dialogue processes. Comprehensive dialogues among political actors in Burundi and the CAR are prime examples (Ofstad, 2012). The dialogue project in the CAR resulted in a national unity government, and although this unity eventually appeared to be weaker than hoped for, the project did illustrate the potential of dialogue.

A general discussion and recommendations on reconciliation processes are offered by Brounéus (2003), and valuable insights into peaceful interaction/dialogue are given in USAID (2011).

The role of media

Media may heighten tensions and induce violence. They may also induce reconciliation. Media can therefore be used both to build and to destroy peace.

Hate media

In tense conflicts some media might actively encourage violence and hatred. In such cases, you may face a dilemma between freedom of speech and the need to contain the conflict. There are, however, certain limits free speech should never be allowed to cross. For example, direct and public incitement to commit genocide is a violation of the United Nations Genocide Convention and should be stopped if possible. One should also observe the International Convention on Elimination of All Forms of Racial Discrimination (paragraph 4), which declares racial propaganda and incitement of racial discrimination to be punishable by law. From a legal point of view one might, in addition, argue that any broadcast or publication that incites violence justifies defence. Stopping such incitements is therefore a relevant means of defence.

Inflammatory radio programmes in Rwanda were probably instrumental in inciting the genocide and would clearly have justified a crackdown. The United Nations Mission commander in Kigali, Major General Dallaire, said that if he had been equipped with proper jamming devices, many lives might have been spared (see Gardner in Reychler and Paffenholz, 2001).

As far as possible, peacebuilders should try to intervene through dialogue, reports or other available means to prevent hate media activities.

Peace media

The purpose of peace media can be defined as promotion of peace through influence of public sentiments. Supporting such activities can be a valuable contribution. But why would people listen to peace media?

Experience suggests that radio broadcasts containing information relevant to people in conflict areas do catch their interest. Topics of interest are refugee issues, immigration, repatriation, humanitarian aid and medical programmes. To the extent that people's attention is caught, possibilities for positive influence open up. Valuable input would, for instance, include dialogue between moderates from each side of the conflict, reports on reconciliation, life stories of people on both sides, cooperation between former enemies, etc.

Depending on people's access to the web, social media such as Twitter and Facebook also hold great potential for information and influence. A striking example is the Arab Spring (see Verghese and Kelly, 2012).

Who may support peace media efforts?

Some UN operations have the means required. For example, the UN Transitional Authority in Eastern Slavonia, Baranja and Western Sirmium had its own TV and radio station in Eastern Slavonia, and UNTAET had radio programmes in East Timor.

From 1992, Search for Common Ground (SCG) and Common Ground Productions (CGP) were among the prime actors in media projects in Macedonia, Bosnia and Burundi. Their approach has varied from training journalists to running radio stations. In Europe, the OSCE might offer support, and local partners may also be available. A good start could be to raise the issue within the peacebuilding community with a view to possible initiatives.

Cooperation between adversaries: lessons from social psychology

Peacebuilders sometimes initiate projects where people from both sides of a conflict are expected to work together. In East Timor, the UN recruited senior police officers from the resistance movement as well as the old police force that had served under Indonesian leadership during the occupation, a fact that unfortunately contributed to the breakdown of the peace process in 2006.[25]

Can we hope to reconcile the parties to a conflict by having them work together? An experiment carried out by the social psychologist Muzafer Sherif and his colleagues in 1961, aimed at testing out group conflict theory, offers interesting perspectives on reconciliation through cooperation (Aronson *et al.*, 1999). Using the setting of a Boy Scout camp, they randomly assigned the participants, a number of 12-year old boys, to one of two groups: the Eagles and the Rattlers. The two groups stayed in separate cabins, and efforts were designed to make each group as cohesive as possible. Both activities and meals were separate. After some time a series of competitions were arranged between the two groups, with prizes for the winning team only. A feeling of tension and conflict began to emerge between the groups. The events culminated with a joint party, prepared by the researchers. Having given the groups different times to start the party, they prepared two kinds of food and refreshments. Half of it was nice and appetising, the other half unattractive. The group that turned up first consumed all the good food, leaving the bad for the others. As the last group turned up and saw what was left, accusations and insults were exchanged, soon developing into fist fights and a full-scale riot.

The investigators now wanted to reverse the process and reconcile the boys. How would they do that? They first arranged a series of non-competitive gatherings, like watching movies together. The hostilities and distrust only continued to rise, however, despite the neutral setting. What eventually brought reconciliation was particular events deftly staged by the investigators. First they arranged for a breakdown of the water supply system, which could only be repaired if all the Rattlers and Eagles cooperated. Next, the camp's truck broke down on a steep hill and all the boys had to pull it to the top together. Now relationships started changing. After a while some of the boys declared that their best friends belonged to the other group.

One might argue that the experiment addressed a conflict that was quite new. Can cooperation reconcile the parties to an old and 'well-established' conflict? A later example from social psychology may offer an answer.

Up to the early 1970s schools in parts of the US had been segregated, so children of different ethnic and racial backgrounds attended different schools. In 1971 the school system of Austin, Texas, was desegregated. White, black and Mexican American children were to attend the same schools. This led to immediate turmoil, fist fights and open hostilities between children with different racial backgrounds. The social psychologist Elliot Aronson was asked for assistance. Bearing in mind the experiences from the boys' camp experiment, he developed a model called the jigsaw class-room. Students were to work in diverse six-person learning groups. The lessons would be divided into six paragraphs, so that each student had one segment of written material, which was a unique and vital part of the total picture. If a group was learning about Eleanor Roosevelt, her biography would be split into six parts, and each student would have to teach the others what he or she had learned. Thus they each depended on the other members of the group to get good marks in the ensuing test. This interdependency changed the climate, leading to friendly probing questions and encouraging remarks in the learning process, and the children gradually started paying more attention and respect to each other. The level of prejudice decreased, and the students improved their self-esteem and achieved better marks.

Aronson observes that one reason for the good result is that the approach broke down in-group versus out-group perceptions. Another was that the cooperative strategy placed people in a favour-doing situation. From the section on cognitive dissonance (pp. 66–68), you may recall that we are inclined to like the people we help.

Based on these and other experiments, it appears possible to establish a set of conditions that has to apply if cooperation efforts are to successfully break down prejudice (Aronson *et al.*, 1999):

1. The participants must have common goals.
2. There must be mutual interdependence. The participants should depend on each other to reach their goals.
3. The participants must have equal status. No one should be boss or subordinate.
4. There must be a friendly informal setting that provides one-to-one contact.
5. There should be multiple friendly contacts with 'typical' representatives from the other group. One must avoid the notion that 'this guy is an exception'.

6 Equality should prevail among the participants. This might be ensured through a professor's influence.

These principles may hold great potential for reconciliation if applied to programmes or projects in post-war areas. Imagine, for instance, reconstruction projects involving a large number of participants from both sides, under professional guidance and in the conditions described above.

Of course, such projects do not hold the answer to all reconciliation challenges. If the problem is systemic, such as a dysfunctional judiciary, you cannot avoid addressing the system. However, whenever there is an opening for cooperation between the parties, there could be possibilities for applying the model.

It is paramount that the cooperation project succeeds. If the parties fail to interact peacefully or fail to reach the common goal, it may worsen the relationship, making them lose faith in reconciliation. This means that if considering such activities, you must make sure that all the conditions are met, throughout the implementation. To ensure success, you might wish to include a social psychologist in addition to the technical experts required.[26]

A needs 'menu'

The above presentation of peacebuilding needs is not complete. Neither is the menu below, even if it is more comprehensive. The idea here is to give you an overview of the peacebuilding activities that are most likely to be of relevance.[27]

1 Restoration of security
Restoration of the military and police
Protection of vulnerable groups
Commissions of inquiry
Training of police and soldiers
Mine clearance
Disarmament
Reintegration of ex-combatants

2 Re/establishment of a legitimate judiciary
Judicial reforms
Re/construction of courts
Training of judges and staff
Police reforms and training

3 Restoration/development of a peace economy
Economic reforms
Development assistance projects
Promotion of inter-communal trade
Agricultural development
Industrial projects

Physical infrastructure such as ports, roads and airports
Electricity supply and telecommunications

4 *Job creation*
Projects ensuring employment for ex-fighters/youth

5 *Sound political development*
Programmes promoting an integrative political climate, 'we-ness' and commitment to cooperation, including dialogue programmes
Constitutional reforms
Election reform
Decentralisation of power
Political institution-building/party-building
Election support and monitoring
Training of civil servants and politicians
Human rights promotion, monitoring and institution building

6 *Restoration/development of the administration*
Re/establishment of the public administration
Training of civil servants

7 *Restoration/development of the education system*
Re/establishment of educational institutions
Education reforms
Training of teachers

8 *Restoration/development of medical services*
Re/construction of hospitals and clinics
Training of medical personnel
Projects addressing special medical needs
Community-based health projects

9 *Peace-oriented information and communication systems*
Nationwide, peace-oriented media coverage
Development of alternative information and communication sources
International broadcasts
Journalist training
Training of politicians

10 *Structures for coping with the problems of refugees and internally displaced persons*
Establishment of support to refugee camps
Housing projects
Resettlement and repatriation

11 *Coverage of immediate humanitarian needs*
Food assistance
Water and sanitation
Shelter
Medical assistance

12 *Reconciliation/conflict resolution*
National community-based reconciliation programmes
Peace and reconciliation commissions

Conflict resolution mechanisms, including restoration and development of new ones
Cooperation projects
Peace education and school programmes
Training of teachers/politicians/civil servants/police/military
Non-violence campaigns
Confidence- and trust-building advocacy
Friendship groups
Cultural exchange
Peace-oriented sports programmes
Exchange programmes for schools, universities, etc.
Shows and festivals for peace
Engaging artists, celebrities and former combatants for peace
Street theatre
Peace media

Planning

'If we do not know where we are going, it is difficult to get there' (Lederach, 1997: 77).

Complex endeavours demand thorough planning, and peacebuilding is no exception. Macro planning is essential, and planning at programme and project level need to be anchored in a strategic framework/overall peacebuilding plans.

The Joint Utstein Study of peacebuilding, which analysed a total of 336 peacebuilding projects implemented by the UK, Germany, the Netherlands, and Norway over a 10-year period, found a major strategic deficiency:

> The problem is visible in the fact that more than 55 per cent of the projects do not show any link to a broader strategy for the country in which they are implemented. Some projects are not linked to a broader strategy because there is no strategy for them to be linked to.
>
> (Smith, 2004: 10)

One might add that projects and programmes should not only be linked to overall strategies, which may at times be general and vague; they should as far as possible fit into concrete peacebuilding plans.

What kinds of plans are needed?

The idea here is not to give a complete recipe for peacebuilding planning, which is normally the responsibility of the government in charge, but some viewpoints seem justified.

The analyses suggested above are essential for the planning process. Such analyses would normally reveal a landscape of complex challenges and comprehensive needs. To address these effectively, one can hardly avoid comprehensive plans that define in clear terms the action required to meet the needs. This is about providing an adequate peacebuilding management tool as well as presenting the peacebuilding needs to the world.

Sector plans would normally be appropriate, covering all sectors of society that are dysfunctional or in need of restoration/development. Typical sectors would be governance, public administration, the judiciary, security, education, health and economy/employment.

A special 'sector plan' might be appropriate for conflict management, meaning activities aimed at conflict resolution and reconciliation. This would differ from other forms of sector planning. While it is possible to determine what you need to establish a parliament or a local health clinic, it is not possible to define specifically what it takes to erase hatred and mistrust.

There may be an array of options ranging from essential activities such as political dialogue projects and mediation between rival groups, to activities that are likely to have positive effects, such as construction of a multicultural centre, joint summer camps for youth from rival ethnic groups, etc.

How far should the plans go in including peace-promoting activities? The view here is that one should cast the net wide. An inadequate national reconciliation programme might doom a peacebuilding process to failure, but there can hardly be too many reconciliation efforts.

In addition to the conflict management activities that are included in the plans, the peacebuilding leadership should in general welcome reconciliation programmes or projects from any actor willing to contribute. If Football 4 Peace International wants to launch a community project, or Search for Common Ground is interested in establishing a peace radio, these may become valuable contributions even if they are not included in an overall plan.

Strategic frameworks and peacebuilding plans may be separate documents or merged. Peacebuilding may also be included in development plans. Adequate government peacebuilding plans are, however, rare. What we find more frequently is a development plan or a poverty reduction strategy.

Since 2006 the UN has helped some governments formulate a priority plan for urgent peacebuilding needs and a joint strategic framework for peacebuilding. However, as we shall see, ownership of such frameworks may be a problem.

Development and poverty reduction plans are primarily focused on reconstruction and economic development. Elements of conflict resolution may be part of the plan, and political dialogue and national reconciliation might be referred to as priorities. So may the establishment of truth and reconciliation commissions. But otherwise the plans would rarely include much on what is needed to achieve national reconciliation.

What should be the time perspective of peacebuilding plans? This depends on their nature. For an overall strategic framework, a perspective of less than five years is hardly realistic. One can in principle imagine a similar time-frame for more concrete peacebuilding plans, including sector plans and definition of programmes needed. Given the often rapidly changing realities on the ground, such long-term planning may be tricky, and regular revisions would be needed.

Whatever the time perspectives of plans, the responsible government must combine long-term perspectives with a readiness to adjust as the needs change.

UN planning

In the rare case of the UN building a state from scratch, such as in East Timor, it will be the UN's responsibility to make adequate peacebuilding plans.

Surprisingly, the UN did not develop an overall peacebuilding plan when the operations started in East Timor. The document coming closest to a plan was the Secretary General's report to the Security Council of 4 October 1999, where some parameters for the activities were presented (S/1999/1024). These parameters were largely borrowed from the UN Kosovo operations (Caplan, 2005: 161). According to senior UN staff, this report was however, no planning document.[28] Major General Michael Smith, who was involved in the planning in New York of the International Force for East Timor (INTERFET) and later engaged in developing the military component of UNTAET, has presented several reasons why UNTAET was 'unable to start its mission with a coherent strategic (corporate) business plan', adding that 'once deployed, the day to day problems further hindered the development of such a plan' (Smith, 2003: 103).

Given the lack of plans for this huge operation, many of the UN achievements, particularly in institution building, were impressive. The component that suffered most from the lack of plans and analysis was probably conflict management.

How does UN peacebuilding planning proceed today, after the establishment of the 2006 UN architecture? A two-step approach has been common. In the Central African Republic, Sierra Leone and Guinea-Bissau, the UN helped the government develop:

- A priority plan.
  This plan would be used as a basis for allocations from the Peacebuilding Fund.
- A framework for peacebuilding.
  The purpose of the framework is to identify peacebuilding objectives that can serve as a shared platform for the government and its partners.

Burundi was also given assistance in the development of these two planning documents, but in addition there was a separate Tracking and Monitoring Mechanism with matrices presenting indicators/benchmarks and commitments.

The plans' specification of needs and action differed. Guinea-Bissau's Priority Plan for the United Nations Peacebuilding Fund included some general peacebuilding priorities, but also four specific 'quick win' projects that the government considered urgent. Burundi's Priority Plan for Peacebuilding included 14 priorities or objectives termed 'projects', many of which were very loosely defined. For example:

- rehabilitation of the role of women in the process of reconstruction and reconciliation;
- mobilising the youth to make them into actors for peace and reconstruction (UN Peacebuilding Fund, 2007).

The Priority Plan offered no guidance on how the rehabilitation of the role of women or the mobilisation of youth was to be organised. Neither did Burundi's strategic Framework for Peacebuilding (PBC/1/BDI/4), nor its Monitoring and Tracking Mechanism. As we shall see below in the section 'Identification of implementing actors' (pp. 137–138), vague parameters may lead to random activities.

While a framework for peacebuilding might be supported by matrices with indicators, benchmarks and commitments, and thus offer a higher degree of direction, one problem is that no one may own such frameworks completely.

In Burundi's *Framework for Peacebuilding* of February 2007 we find 'Transitional Justice', an objective expressly related to mechanisms of national reconciliation, which the Priority Plan had described as the basis for peacebuilding in Burundi (UN Peacebuilding Fund, 2007; UN Peacebuilding Commission, 2007). This was to include both provisions for transitional justice and a national reconciliation commission. However, as indicated above, in January 2014 there was still no Truth and Reconciliation Commission in Burundi, and no transitional justice. There was disagreement between the government and the UN about the justice component, and this may have prevented implementation (Ofstad, 2012).

In Liberia in 2011, the government and the UN developed a joint Liberia Peacebuilding Programme instead of a Framework for Peacebuilding. The joint programme is a more thorough and detailed planning document, more specific in its definition of expected results and indicators, and includes indicative budget figures (UN Peacebuilding Fund, 2011). The plan does, however, build on a Priority Plan for Peacebuilding, which basically defines the government's priorities but without the kind of conflict analysis suggested here.

We shall not embark on an analysis of the UN's planning support to governments. However, it seems fair to suggest that a thorough assessment of the UN planning support following the 2006 reforms is called for.

The UN usually makes its own plans for peacebuilding support to the government. UNDAF, a document agreed between the UN and the government, is such a plan, describing the different UN agencies' responsibilities.

Moreover, with a view to ensuring coherence between UN peace missions and UN country teams, the Integrated Approach was adopted in 2008, requiring a shared vision, aligned planning, agreed results, timelines and responsibilities, and mechanisms for monitoring and evaluation (see de Coning, 2009).

Budgeting

Peacebuilding plans should be accompanied by at least an indicative budget, covering all sectors and activities deemed necessary for the duration of the plan.

(The New Deal commits to what is termed three-to-five-year indicative forward estimates.)

A realistic picture of costs is essential, and to the extent that there is a concrete plan, all components need to be budgeted, meaning there should be budget figures for all sectors and programme component parts. A substantial contingency line should be provided for opportunities that are not apparent in the beginning.

Like the peacebuilding plan, the budget should be subject to regular revisions.

Presentation

Presentation influences the international community's response. The stage of international assistance is a competitive place, and long-term peacebuilding needs compete with needs related to natural disasters as well as with non-conflict-related development aid requirements.

Donor conferences

A common approach is to hold an early donor conference, where an overview of the challenges is presented and international society is requested to pledge support.

With today's media and communication tools, such conferences may offer excellent presentation opportunities, for example structured, big screen presentations of needs which highlight specific figures for sectors like justice, governance, security, education, health and more. GIS resources can be used to create maps and tables that illustrate the spread of the needs in the country as a whole or at regional, district and village level.

The prevalence of conflicts may also be graphically illustrated by symbols and figures, as may the location of governmental and possible peacebuilding structures or organisations present in the country. The support expected from various donors may also be mapped, with graphic illustration of the gaps between needs and coverage. This allows for some amount of adaptation early on, and the same documentation can be posted on the internet and later serve as a basis for coordination (pp. 139–143).

A well-prepared conference may offer opportunities for plenary discussions as well as topic-based group work and bilateral discussion of possible cooperation.

Unfortunately, while the technical potential to make the presentations suggested above is available, the general failure to provide comprehensive needs – and conflict analysis (discussed on pp. 109–112) – prevents its full realisation.

Appeals

While humanitarian needs are often presented in international appeals, the same has not been the case for peacebuilding needs.

If we use the five-year planning approach indicated as a possibility above, we could in principle imagine one comprehensive appeal covering all peacebuilding needs discussed in this book for a five-year period with possible extensions.

Even if the New Deal suggests three-to-five year indicative estimates, five-year peacebuilding appeals may not be seen anytime soon. But apparently the world is slowly shedding the illusion that a few selective efforts towards institution building, security and economic development for a one-to-two year period can be enough to build lasting peace. For a better understanding of how UN appeals work today, see UNDG/ECHA's Guidance Note on Funding for Transition of 2009.[29]

Websites

Any peacebuilding operation should have a website containing possible appeals, analyses, plans, progress reports and all other information that may be of interest to donors.

While UN peacebuilding operations normally have websites, much of the above information may be missing. Governments in charge of peacebuilding rarely have adequate websites. If your organisation is planning to give peacebuilding support to a war-torn country, you may have great difficulty finding essential information, and important documents may not be available in English. Helping governments to establish and run appropriate peacebuilding websites is therefore a challenge to organisations with the capacity to do so.

Identification of implementing actors

Let us assume there is an adequate peacebuilding plan, defining a substantial number of activities. Who is to implement them?

Ideal implementation would imply a structured distribution of tasks among capable actors. As we know, this is not how it works. While the UN, the Bretton Woods system and other institutional donors do cooperate with governments, most other international organisations decide what to do and where quite independently.

Still, in some contexts governments are involved in the identification of implementing actors. The two programmes managed by the World Bank in East Timor, the multi-donor Trust Fund for East Timor (TFET) and the Transition Support Programme (TSP), are examples. Once the government was established in 2002, it was actively involved in the selection of suitable implementers.

The UN architecture of 2006 provided another facility that involves governments in the identification process. Countries found eligible are granted a lump sum from the Peacebuilding and Recovery Facility to address needs identified in the government's Priority Plan for Peacebuilding, and in-country allocations from this grant are decided by a Joint Steering Committee. Co-chaired by the national government and the UN, the Steering Committee invites members of the UN family to present proposals from partner organisations.

How does this work? There is little analysis available, but in Burundi an external evaluation of grants from the Peacebuilding Fund was conducted in March 2010, offering some thought-provoking criticism. While acknowledging that some innovative activities were funded, the team found that overall strategic guidance was missing and that the selection process suffered from a lack of conceptual clarity.

> After many hours of debate, the Committee of Experts selected 18 projects in a wide range of sectors. While these projects could all arguably qualify as peacebuilding projects, this evaluation found that they were in fact not all appropriate for the timeframe and expected outcomes of PBF funding.
>
> (Campbell *et al.*, 2010)

The problem of managing international support

Outside the realm of trust funds and cooperation with institutional donors, the government generally has limited influence on what international actors do. What are the reasons for this? Three factors seem to stand out.

Lack of resources

War-ravaged countries generally have limited financial and human resources, whereas external actors bring in both. This makes it difficult for the governments to exert control.

Lack of regulatory framework

Most states have no legislation defining how peacebuilding support and/or humanitarian operations should be managed.

Indonesia's draft Disaster Response Law, developed after the operational chaos that followed the tsunami of December 2004, stated that foreign actors wanting to render humanitarian support would have to present their plans to the government and get them endorsed before starting their work. If we assume that there is a competent and effective body processing plans, possibly with the support of the UN, such an approach could go some way to ensuring relevant peacebuilding activities.

The International Federation of Red Cross and Red Crescent Societies has since 2007 advocated development of indigenous legislation that would lay down norms for the management of large-scale disasters, part of the purpose being to ensure indigenous leadership vis-à-vis international actors. While many governments understand the need, few have taken steps to develop the required legislation.

As observed above, all peacebuilders should, regardless of the regulatory framework, consult with the peacebuilding leadership and present ideas and plans to local authorities. This way we may not only avoid contributing to chaos, but also show basic respect for the host country and earn respect for our agency.

Lack of leadership capacity

The leaders of a war-torn country may have little knowledge of peacebuilding. We have touched upon the problem of lack of analysis and adequate planning, which is partly related to lack of such capacity. Another essential capacity that might be missing is the ability to lead the process and coordinate. While a general discussion of leadership is beyond the scope of this book, coordination is a core issue. Without analysis, plans and a regulatory framework, essential parameters will be missing, and coordination can indeed be demanding. So let us take a closer look at it.

Coordination

This is an essential macro element but is also important in micro contexts. If there are a large number of international and local actors, how can peacebuilding be implemented in a coherent and structured way?[30]

Given that non-institutional donors normally decide what to do and where to do it for themselves, there is a risk of chaos where organisations get in each other's way in 'hot' areas and leave needier ones without support. This problem is even more pronounced in hectic disaster response efforts than in peace operations. Without proper coordination we may see huge amounts of financial and human resources spent in haphazard ways.

But what is coordination really about?

The essence

The purpose of peacebuilding, as well as of development aid and emergency operations, is to meet needs.

The essence of coordination is to adapt, integrate and facilitate activities towards the most effective needs coverage possible. That is, we need to know what needs exist and where. We should keep track at all times of what remains unaddressed as we progress with needs coverage.

If we imagine a scenario where adequate analysis and planning have taken place, we will have a good overall picture of the needs and know the government's priorities. Even so, the overall picture may include limited data on the situation on the ground, and additional field assessments may be required to define what is needed where.

Coordination forums and peacebuilding leadership should at all times have updated figures and information on needs available, specific enough to serve as a basis for activities. Any discussion of action should take place against this background. Only with such information can we undertake informed assessments of what action is needed and ascertain how to address all the requirements at once.

If you inform a coordination forum that you are starting a protection project for 500 people in a certain region, that is probably good per se, but what does it mean in terms of needs coverage?

Are you covering all the protection needs or could there be 5,000 more people with similar needs in the area? Could there be more urgent needs elsewhere? The example may sound exaggerated, but international coordination forums are often weighed down by such a lack of clarity.

As mentioned, organisations may flock to central places where they compete over project opportunities and visibility, but this is sometimes also attributable to a lack of knowledge about the needs landscape.

To facilitate cooperation on needs coverage, coordinators should at any time be able to present overhead maps of the country or region in question, showing both a sectoral (justice, food, security, health, etc.) and a geographical breakdown of needs.

Such maps may also show where different agencies are working and, equally important, where they are not. The needs coverage figures should be updated as a running process.

Population patterns, density and movements may be illustrated by maps, as may infrastructure and logistical data (roads, bridges, rivers, warehouses, schools, churches/mosques, etc.) as well as potential security threats.

Unfortunately, this kind of peacebuilding coordination has hardly ever taken place, despite the availability of GIS and rich IT possibilities. The peacebuilding community has not yet exploited the possibilities that today's technology offers, and/or invested in the manpower required to map and monitor the needs thoroughly throughout the operation.

Some promising developments are found in disaster management context,[31] but most international coordination forums lack the essential background of well-documented and updated needs. Admittedly, needs mapping/updates may demand a lot of resources, but without such investment, an essential part of the basis for coordination will remain missing.

With this in mind, how useful can coordination be? Luckily, even if the overall needs picture is missing or incomplete, we may have knowledge, particularly in local contexts, that renders mutual support, information exchange and integration possible. This may range from whatever we know about the needs in question, to political developments, project data, information on security developments and practical issues of interest. There are also issues of principle related to our work that call for discussion. With this in mind, international actors should at all times be ready to discuss the following questions:

- How do we share relevant information and experiences?
- Should we split areas between us geographically?
  Geographical division sometimes make operations more effective.
- Should we complement each other's activities?
  If one organisation is providing food to a vulnerable village, another may have a surplus of blankets, another a stock of needed medicines, etc.
- Should we make joint action plans?
  This may be appropriate if we are working in the same area or addressing the same conflict from different angles.

- Should we cooperate on logistics?
  All organisations in the field have vehicles. Should we pool them in the event of urgent needs?
- Should we join forces on particular initiatives?
  For example, organisations concerned about human rights abuse in the police, sometimes 'gang up' on the political or police leadership.
- Can we help each other with introductions to local connections?
  Organisations involved in a project with the local administration may sometimes introduce and support other organisations which need to cooperate with the same administration.
- Can we share/rationalise our work and/or utilise opportunities jointly?
  You may recall the police training seminars run jointly by the UNHCR and the OSCE about policing in a democracy (p. 83). At times the UN police also contributed with training in police ethics. Thus, three organisations used the same practical arrangement.
- Should we develop a peace infrastructure together (see below)?
  If this is of interest, one might discuss both work and cost sharing.
- Can we cooperate on ensuring long-term effects?
  This includes the aspect of sustainability, ensuring local take-over, continuity among international actors and more.
- Should we discuss the 'Do no harm' concept (pp. 148–151)?
  While needs coverage is the purpose of our work, it is also important to avoid negative effects.

If you happen to be in charge of coordination, you might present all these questions to the participants, for instance by power point or in an early memo. It may not all be accepted/used, but the point is to create discussion and awareness of possibilities. Again, only the imagination sets the limit as to the possibilities for cooperation.

However, a number of factors could frustrate cooperation. Hostility among the conflicting parties is one. If peacebuilding organisations A and B are working with villages in conflict, the atmosphere of hostility may reduce A's and B's scope of cooperation.

Differences in the various organisations' mode of operation can also be an obstacle. Some work long term, some short term. Some have the financial and regulatory freedom to cooperate with others, some do not. Commitments to donors may oblige organisations to 'go it alone', as they have to show concretely what has been achieved with the donors' money.

As observed earlier, your agency's freedom may be limited by your strategic frameworks, and also those of other organisations. An example mentioned earlier (p. 101) is the EU's voluntary code of conduct for a better division of labour between the EU donors in developing countries (EU, 2007). While aimed at complementarity in development aid, this code's general principles of cooperation may also influence your freedom to cooperate in a peacebuilding context.[32]

Still, whatever norms and allegiances international actors have to observe, most delegates attending coordination forums do so with the desire to cooperate, and the challenge is to make the best of the freedom we have.

Who should coordinate?

If the UN is building a state from scratch as in the case of East Timor, coordination should be part of its responsibility. Surprisingly, with the exception of a public health group, the UN initiated no overall coordination among humanitarian actors outside the UN family.

If a government is in charge, coordination is its responsibility. However, given lack of capacity, the government may depend on the UN for supporting the coordination of assistance. In any case, the UN should offer to help the government coordinate the international agencies' activities.

There might be a UN Special Representative of the Secretary General holding this responsibility. It might also be the task of the UN Resident Coordinator, normally the head of the UNDP.

In countries where the UN Office for the Coordination of Humanitarian Aid (OCHA) is represented, it is supposed to 'mobilise and coordinate effective and principled humanitarian action in partnership with national and international actors'.[33] However, OCHA has not assumed the role of coordinator in peacebuilding operations.

What about other international organisations? Other than the UN, and the World Bank in donor contexts, no organisations stand out as coordinators of international actors in the field. On p. 32 we suggested regular meetings for international organisations, but sometimes no one takes the initiative needed. You might perhaps convene the first meeting?

Can local organisations help with coordination? One example of a local entity contributing to coordination is the Community Relations Council in Northern Ireland (p. 108), which served as a databank and a forum for interaction/discussions.

In a war-torn area, there may not be any local organisations ready to take on such challenges. International delegates should anyhow see it as a challenge to invite and involve local actors at the earliest possible stage.

Peace infrastructure

Peacebuilding should ideally include well-integrated, multi-sector efforts at all levels of society. To ensure this, some writers suggest an infrastructure for peace, meaning a network of actors strategically positioned at different levels and sectors. Supposedly such cooperation will contribute to cross-fertilisation of ideas and synergy effects.

One concern is that this requires time and resources.

Even if peacebuilding often involves many resources, much is left to be desired in terms of cooperation, and someone will have to cover the expenses and do the work. That is, someone must convene meetings, set up agendas, distribute information, etc.

It is easy to agree that in general such a network might be very useful. If the establishment of a national network is too ambitious, you might still assess the possibilities of a regional or local one.

Monitoring

The needs identified through analysis and addressed through proper planning will necessarily change with time, and must therefore be updated. This requires monitoring. To monitor effectively, we need baseline data, but given the common lack of analysis discussed above, such data may never have been collected in a sufficiently structured manner.

For adequate monitoring to take place, the peacebuilding leadership should allocate it ample resources and personnel at an early stage.

Despite the general lack of such resource allocation, monitoring may be useful, subject to topic and scope. If you know how many schools were destroyed during a war, it may be easy to follow the progress of reconstruction, and if there was no functioning judiciary, you may be able to observe the appointment of judges and the number of cases being processed.

But what about the development of peace? If applying peace and conflict indicators, you may be able to keep tabs on associated developments.

Peace indicators are data related to positive developments, such as:

- increased employment
- trade
- school enrolment
- return of refugees
- ex-fighters reintegrated
- disarmament.

Conflict indicators are data reflecting developments that threaten peace, such as:

- violent incidents
- cases of extortion
- corruption reports
- incidents of discrimination
- demonstrations/civil unrest
- armed group movements or developments.

As part of an analytical support programme to the peace process in Aceh, called the Conflict and Community Development Programme, the World Bank applied a newspaper conflict mapping methodology to record and categorise all incidents of conflict reported in two provincial newspapers (*Serambi* and *Aceh Kita*). The programme published monthly updates and analysis of the data, complemented by field work where possible, in both English and Indonesian.[34]

The World Bank's effort represents one interesting model. A more traditional approach is regular collection and processing of reports from field staff. Most international organisations have reporting routines that allow for some collection of data. However, the processing of data, which enables continuous observation of developments, is often missing.

The peacebuilding leadership should establish reporting routines ensuring that essential monitoring data are processed and available as a basis for analysis and possible adjustments. The possibilities of GIS, IT and social media should be explored.

Evaluations/adjustments

A conflict landscape may change quickly, as may the needs related to peacebuilding. To ensure the relevance of the peacebuilding process, the need for adjustments and changes should be reviewed regularly.

In East Timor, there were significant changes during the early years of the peacebuilding process. Scambary (2009) provides a thought-provoking analysis of rivalries, animosities and loyalties, showing a number of baffling changes. Trinidade and Castro (2007) observes that there was a significant movement of young men to the cities of East Timor, and that nearly all the 2006 violence took place in the cities. As violence is in general more likely in a young population, monitoring this development might have been useful.

We may have limited resources to monitor, and little influence on changes that take place. But we should always do our best to access and update relevant facts and make the analyses/evaluations we are able to. We must be ready to adjust along the way and learn from our experiences. Programmes should normally be subjected to at least mid-term and end evaluations.

For a guide on evaluation of peacebuilding activities, see OECD/DAC (2012), *Evaluating Peacebuilding Activities in Settings of Conflict and Fragility*.

Programming

Programming in our terminology means defining action to meet needs. For our purpose we may divide needs into two categories.

Needs pertaining to a dysfunctional society

The macro question here is: if we are to ensure peace, how must the society's institutions and structures look and function? As indicated, adequate sector plans should outline all the activities needed to take us there.

All programming related to the restoration/development of institutions and structures should be based on an overall peacebuilding plan and/or development plans. If no such plans exist, ensuring relevance may be a challenge, but as observed above, the least we can do is to present our ideas and plans to the peacebuilding leadership/local authorities for assessment/ discussion.

Needs pertaining to conflict

The world has not got very far in working out how to reduce large-scale antagonism. Truth and reconciliation commissions have proved effective in some countries, but they depend on extensive voluntary participation, which is not always attainable. Imagination is, however, an important resource for peacebuilding and, in general, we need to explore all opportunities for reconciliation with an open mind.

Let us look at some factors/resources that we may draw on/observe in programming contexts.

Connectors/dividers

Anderson (1999) emphasises the use of 'connectors', meaning aspects that have been known to connect or bring people closer, for example the restoration of a market place where the parties used to trade peacefully (see p. 151).

'Dividers', on the other hand, factors that set people apart, could be harmful in a programming context. For instance, if there are strong prejudices between two groups, bringing them together in a joint programme without precautions might be disastrous. (On the breakdown of prejudices, see p. 128.)

Groups and people with no active role in a conflict sometimes assume active roles in peacebuilding efforts, and exploring such possibilities may prove rewarding.

Religious leaders/community leaders

It is worth exploring whether local leaders are willing to participate in peace and reconciliation work.

In East Timor, the Church was a strong unifying symbol during much of the Indonesian occupation. When peace came, the Church was not invited to become a partner in the peacebuilding process, and a serious conflict subsequently emerged between the Church and the government.

Known personalities/artists

Most societies have celebrities and persons widely admired or respected. Whatever their claim to fame, respected and admired persons can be very valuable in peace campaigns. Musicians, singers and other artists sometimes undertake significant efforts for reconciliation.

Women

UN Security Council Resolution 1325 of 2000 generally calls for women's equal participation in peace processes, both nationally and internationally. More specifically it calls on 'all actors involved, when negotiating and implementing peace agreements, to adopt a gender perspective', including, inter alia, 'measures that support local women's peace initiatives and indigenous processes for conflict resolution, and that involve women in all of the implementation mechanisms of the peace agreements'.

The International Crisis Group's research in Sudan, the Congo (DRC) and Uganda suggests that:

> peace agreements, post-conflict reconstruction, and governance do better when women are involved. Women make a difference, in part because they adopt a more inclusive approach toward security and address key social and economic issues that would otherwise be ignored.[35]

While there is a growing realisation that women represent an under-utilised force in peacebuilding contexts, both governments and external peacebuilders often ignore women as a resource/possible actors.

Ex-combatants

Engaging former fighters for peace may be a powerful tool. Many have experienced horrors that change their mindset for ever, and some will be willing to talk about it. Former fighters talking about peace and war, for instance in schools, can make a difference, particularly if combatants from different sides of the conflict do it together.

Youth

While youth are commonly used and abused as fighters, they may also contribute to peace. Possible alleys are peace forums and meetings for youth, involvement of youth in peaceful political processes and dialogue/peace advocacy projects. Youth initiatives may sometimes find support in international networks, such as Youth against Violence in South America.[36]

While involving large numbers of young people may be very resource-demanding, positively engaged youth leaders may have considerable impact on their peers.

Children

We are used to the concept of children as victims of war, but they may also be a resource for peace. Anderson (1999) mentions a magazine published by UNICEF for children in Lebanon containing messages of peace and reconciliation, inviting letters from children and offering them a chance to understand children from other ethnic groups. 'Rings in the water' can spread this way, and may influence the attitudes of future youth and adults.

The list of possible actors for peace could surely be extended. Only our imagination sets a limit. The exploration of connectors, discussed at the end of this chapter, may also help us identify new and significant actors for peace.

Conflict impact assessment

Conflict impact assessment (CIAS) is a structured way to assess the influence aid and peacebuilding activities have on conflicts. It may be used on three levels:

- policy level – as part of an analysis of a country or region;
- sector level – focusing on a chosen area of aid or peacebuilding (for example, humanitarian aid or environmental cooperation);
- project or programme level.

The UNDG/ECHA conflict analysis model includes conflict impact assessment at all levels. Doing a thorough CIAS could involve a lot of time and resources. Reychler (Reychler and Paffenholz, 2001), whose framework we draw on here, suggests in-depth interviews and discussions, questionnaires and problem-solving workshops, discussions with staff and involvement of beneficiaries.

However, given the normal workload in the field, most international workers would be happy if they could arrange one small-scale weekend workshop for this purpose. If you hold a conflict analysis workshop (p. 113), a CIAS might be a natural part of this.

In case you decide to do a CIAS workshop, make sure you invite representatives of beneficiaries and project partners. Whether you do it as a joint exercise or part of your programming, you might use the following checklist.

1 What are your goals?
Defining goals and objectives is a natural part of programming. If your activities are likely to render a peace dividend, you may wish to include it in your objectives. For instance, if you are establishing a school, would it be natural to include the end of educational discrimination in the area as an objective?
2 How and to what extent does the project contribute to the goals of the overall peacebuilding plan/development strategy? Even assuming that an adequate peacebuilding plan has been developed, this may be a difficult assessment, but we should attempt it.
3 How will the conflict influence the project?
For example, will there be threats or violence influencing the process? Will there be thefts? Will roads be open and safe? Will labour power from the different sides of the conflict/s be available?
4 What impact is the project going to have on the conflict?
For examples, will it influence negotiation processes or political developments? Will it cause envy/rivalry? Will it reinforce front lines? Will it

influence traditional structures or processes? Will there be reconciliation effects? Is there a risk of supporting a war economy? Will it influence ethics/morals?

5 What will the situation be like at the completion of the programme? Can local actors take over when our organisation withdraws? What are the likely long-term effects?

The CIAS could be laid down in a separate study or integrated in a project document.

Reychler (in Reychler and Paffenholz, 2001) recommends that a CIAS be done before, during and after implementation of a project. Without questioning the desirability of such a comprehensive approach, most busy field staff would be happy if they can do it once, before the implementation.

Indirect effects on peace: the 'Do no harm' concept

As a delegate you may be involved in the distribution of aid. And even if you aren't, you should know something about the effects of aid on conflicts.

Anderson's book *Do No Harm* (1999) is based on research results from the project Local Capacities for Peace, where a number of agencies joined forces to understand how aid and conflict interact. The following observations from *Do No Harm* present valuable peacebuilding perspectives:

Effects of resource transfer

Aid resources can be stolen

Stolen provisions may be used to sustain combatants or sold to finance warfare. Suggested remedies are:

- to deliver aid unannounced or very quickly, perhaps also secretly;
- to disperse transport vehicles along different routes;
- to develop joint strategies with local communities to thwart theft (for example, bring an elderly tribe member as an escort, provided he/she enjoys general respect);
- to lower resale value without damaging usefulness, for example by damaging or removing parts of packages like the lids of oil cans, making holes in rice bags, or cutting blankets in two. (Such blankets can be stitched together by the beneficiaries, but are difficult to sell.)

Aid affects markets

War gives rise to manufacturers who sustain warfare by producing parts or products for the weapons industry or provisions for warring parties. Others benefit because they control assets that donors need. The international community's appearance leads to price hikes on hotel rooms, offices, housing, furniture and other equipment. International organisations also create jobs and pay salaries, often with inflationary effects. In this manner, those who benefit from the international community's presence have an economic interest in continued war. Aid agencies sometimes bring in provisions from abroad that destroy the market for the normal local produce. Rice is, for example, sometimes imported in large quantities even if available locally. Suggested remedies are:

- to avoid dealing with manufacturers or vendors who supply warlords;
- to buy provisions such as agricultural produce from local providers whose business is founded in the normal peacetime economy;
- to avoid bidding up prices and heating up the local economy by assessing the possibility of agreeing fixed prices and rates with other agencies;
- to fix wages at a decent (not war profit) rate;
- to provide training, soft loans and other assistance to local staff with a view to self-sustenance and independence after you have left;
- to discuss negative effects and how to avoid them with the local community.

Distribution impacts

Aid normally targets the neediest groups. This well-meant differentiation might create tension in conflict areas. Groups who don't benefit may become frustrated. They may have undiscovered needs themselves or consider the beneficiaries undeserving.

A suggested remedy is to involve the local community in discussions and decisions on aid distribution. Religious forums or tribal elders may be involved or special committees may be established for this purpose. Experience shows that people involved in a decision-making process tend to show responsibility and favour the neediest regardless of group affiliation. Remember the significance of role expectations (p. 60).

If you are dealing with a conflict between two vulnerable groups, the 'Do no harm' remedy may not be accepted and identifying the neediest subsets can be difficult. What if one or more groups is slightly less needy than the other(s)? Agencies sometimes feel justified in compromising a little on the 'neediest principle' and distribute aid to all groups in a conflict in order to avoid fuelling antagonism.

Substitution effects on aid

If the international community meets important civilian needs like food, shelter and medicines, local resources may be freed for warfare. Warlords may limit their own role to military control, and abandon all responsibility for people's welfare. Suggested remedies are:

- to limit aid to a minimum, not fully meeting needs;
- to support local efforts to meet local needs;
- to encourage warriors to assume responsibility.

Relating to warlords

Warlords are inclined to use their power to impose their own rules or demands on aid agencies. Typical are taxes and duties, their own currency exchange rates and restrictions as to delivery sites and schedules. Humanitarian workers may not have the power to oppose warlords' norms, but you could be in a position where you have to exert influence by peaceful means.

A suggested remedy is to co-opt commanders into taking responsibility for civilian welfare. The idea is to avoid supporting what is illegal while at the same time seeking the commander's support of legitimate purposes. Some aid workers set a 'tone' in the interactions that emphasises tolerance, respect, trust and commitment to human welfare. To co-opt commanders into assuming responsibility for civilian welfare, they set up systems and routines to involve warriors in bettering people's lives. For example, they meet regularly with commanders and their representatives to discuss their aid to civilians; they take 'authorities' to visit project sites so that they can interact with people face to face; and they expose commanders to the real impact of their policies on people's lives.

Anderson (1999) admits that it is difficult to do this without naivety. For your part, you will benefit from the techniques discussed in Chapter 5 above, particularly those pertaining to role expectations and cognitive dissonance. It can, however, require a delicate balance to avoid cooperation that renders authority to the warlord.

Ethical messages

'Do no harm' suggests that a number of ethical messages have been found to exacerbate the negative impact of aid on conflicts:

1 The use of armed guards tends to legitimise the use of arms to determine access to food, health and other services aid agencies provide.
2 Lack of cooperation or conflicts between agencies suggest one does not have to work with or respect people with whom one does not agree.
3 Illegitimate use of aid resources sends a signal of impunity, reflecting warlord attitudes.
4 Emergency plans which show no concern for local employees indicate different values for different lives.
5 Statements like 'It's not my fault; my headquarters makes me do it this way' reflect attitudes frequent in wars, negating personal responsibility.
6 Approaching checkpoints or interacting with warriors with hostility, suspicion and belligerence reinforces the atmosphere prevalent among conflicting groups.
7 Depicting horrors in ways that show that only one side is to blame are seldom accurate and support one-sidedness.

Connectors and dividers

The points above are to a large extent about what (Anderson, 1999) calls dividers, factors that create distances between people and intensify or deepen conflicts. When intervening for peace it is our obligation to try to avoid or abate divisive effects.

As mentioned above, Anderson presents connectors as aspects that are known to connect or bring people closer. A functioning shared market place may be one such element. Even in internal wars we find such aspects.

Connectors may include history and culture, trade, language, joint sports events, educational cooperation, road connections, economic interdependence, communication, joint administrative structures and more.

While *Do No Harm* does not discuss the identification of new connectors, it contains stories from real life where the applied connectors were obviously new. (A peace magazine for children in Lebanon is one such example.)

We should certainly look for ways of strengthening existing connectors, but also look for new ones. Connector initiatives are in principle unlimited. Remember what we have observed about imagination and brainstorming as resolution tools. This is a context where such skills are invaluable.

In general, all peacebuilding/development efforts should, as far as possible, be implemented in a way that strengthens connectors and weakens dividers, whatever the scope or objective.

If you choose to do a conflict analysis (p. 113), this aspect should be included.

Please also remember the recommendation to draw on connectors and observe dividers in programming (p. 145).

Summing up on peacebuilding

The overall picture

- Peacebuilding is about addressing needs, and to address them we have to know them. Thorough analysis is needed to understand the complexities of a post-violence society, and conflict analysis is essential, but neither the UN nor governments in charge of peacebuilding have been providing what is needed. A comprehensive multidisciplinary approach is suggested.
- Complex endeavours need thorough planning. However, government plans rarely address peacebuilding needs adequately. While the 2006 UN architecture brought increased planning support to governments, the value of this support needs to be assessed.
- A review of allocations from the UN Peacebuilding Fund to Burundi raises essential questions about the allocation process, including lack of overall guidance.
- UN peacebuilding should be based on realistic time-frames, plans and budgets. While there is growing understanding of the time aspect of peacebuilding, the usual time-frame for UN operations is still one year at a time.

The 2006 UN architecture, which is not operational, however, sets a wider time-frame. The World Bank is committed to seeking longer-term funding, and the New Deal commits to three-to-five year indicative forward estimates.

- Overall peacebuilding leadership is essential and is normally the government's responsibility. The UN has a general responsibility for peace and security. East Timor is the only case of UN state-building from scratch. The UN operations' mandates did not ensure the overall peacebuilding leadership needed, even when building a new state. The World Bank took a lead role in economic development, which is an important peacebuilding component. Rivalry between the UN and the World Bank was observed, and analysis/reform seems needed.
- The UN operations' mandates are generally inconsistent on reconciliation. If included, reconciliation is normally limited to support for local initiatives. There is generally no active role defined for the UN, a fact possibly influenced by some nations' concerns about UN interference with developing countries.
- The UN may do a great job in institution building, security provision and to some extent economic development, while also facilitating dialogue/conflict resolution. However, the need for large-scale reconciliation is rarely adequately addressed and governments scarcely have the will and/or the capacity required. Important conflict aspects may not be addressed due to lack of analysis/understanding.
- As a matter of principle, the UN seeks to attach truth and reconciliation commissions to transitional justice. However, governments in post-war states are often opposed to the justice component, and the affected people might therefore get neither justice nor reconciliation.
- The 'Needs "menu"' (pp. 130–132) includes a range of possible reconciliation activities that are rarely applied.
- Social psychology offers knowledge about the reconciliation effects of cooperation between adversaries. This knowledge has not been utilised much in peacebuilding and holds interesting perspectives.
- The essence of coordination is to adapt, integrate and facilitate activities towards the most effective needs coverage. The general lack of needs mapping/analysis implies limited knowledge of the needs. There is also a lack of legislative frameworks that could define and strengthen governments' leadership role. Still, coordination might provide useful information sharing and mutual support.
- The UN sometimes fails to coordinate with other international actors.
- Effective monitoring and adjustment of peacebuilding activities are essential. Lack of analysis, strategic planning and knowledge of needs are also obstacles in this regard, as is the lack of investment in monitoring capacity.

Your challenges

- Whether you are involved at a macro or micro level, you should do your best to address the need for adequate analysis and planning. Take the initiative that your position allows. You might do your own conflict analysis, or plan a joint field workshop, addressing your organisation's work context.

- Your organisation should assess how and where it can make the best contribution to peace. This is about geography and level of society as well as specific needs.
- Present ideas and plans to the local government/peacebuilding leadership for discussion/endorsement to ensure alignment with peacebuilding or development priorities and the efforts of other actors as far as possible.
- Be conscious of what kind of peace you are helping to build. Developments/changes of society should be needed, understood and wanted by the local community.
- Has the UN established coordination among international actors? If not, are you in a position to take an initiative? Are there local actors who might play a role in coordination? All organisations should contribute to coordination in their work context.
- Initiate cooperation with local actors as far as possible, and keep in mind the need for a gradual transition.
- All programming should be based on or include a conflict impact assessment.
- Your programmes should be evaluated at intervals and adjusted when needed.
- Even if your activities in the country are not part of peacebuilding, but a contribution to non-conflict-related relief or development, do take time to assess your plans in the perspective of a war/peace economy, as suggested under the 'Do no harm' concept.
- Remember the aspect of connectors and dividers. How can your agency contribute to reconciliation and avoid negative effects on conflicts?

Notes

1 www.usaid.gov/what-we-do/working-crises-and-conflict/technical-publications.
2 For example, SIDA (2012).
3 The report also observed the fragile and conflict-affected states' higher rates of crime, lower life expectancy and lack of basic health care and education.
4 Interestingly, a principle underscored in Busan was that developing countries 'must design and drive their own development' (*Oxfam Briefing Note*, 2012, http://policy-practice.oxfam.org.uk/publications/busan-in-a-nutshell-what-next-for-the-global-partnership-for-effective-developm-245001).
5 www.pbsbdialogue.org/documentupload/03%20PSG%20Indicators%20EN.pdf.
6 See de Coning and de Carvalho (2013).
7 The report refers to International Country Risk Guide indicators from 1985 to 2009.
8 See the World Bank website *Fragility and Conflict. Setting the Paradigm.* (http://siteresources.worldbank.org/EXTLICUS/Resources/sixpoints-brochure.pdf).
9 The UN did initiate reconciliation efforts, but not to the extent needed, and the point here is that the mandate should have been clear from the start. See Ofstad (2012).
10 Co-managed by the Asian Development Bank.

11 There were 222 projects in 22 countries as per January 2013 (www.unpbf.org/).
12 An exception was a coordination forum for organisations involved in health activities.
13 The International Federation of Red Cross and Red Crescent Societies, *Appeal and 1st Programme Update for Sierra Leone, 2002*. (This is no longer available on the web.)
14 The figures vary, but some writers suggest up to 50 per cent relapse in the first five years. See Biersteker (2007).
15 A striking illustration of how conflict equations changed in a volatile phase in East Timor is offered by Scambary (2009).
16 International aspects seem increasingly important in armed conflicts. Prominent examples are Iraq, Afghanistan, Syria and Ukraine. For a discussion of this topic see Ramsbotham, *et al* (2011).
17 http://web.worldbank.org/WBSITE/EXTERNAL/TOPICS/EXTSOCIALDEVELOPMENT/EXTCPR/0,,contentMDK:20486708~menuPK:1260893~pagePK:148956~piPK:216618~theSitePK:407740,00.html. Since 2011, the Bank has also started helping governments of fragile states conduct fragility assessments, identifying challenges to the five peace and statebuilding goals of the New Deal.
18 Telephone interview with C. Wilson, author of the report, by Ofstad in May 2013.
19 *Priority Plan for Peacebuilding in Burundi, Strategic Note 1, Febuary 2007*, www.peacebuilderscenter.jp/parts/20101213–17/20101214Material_Takeuchi.pdf; and *République Centraficaine: Plan prioritaire pour la consolidation de la paix, juin 2008*, www.unpbf.org/docs/CAR_Priority_Plan%20_French_June08.pdf.
20 E. Solheim, Chairman of the OECD Development Assistance Committee (16 May 2013), www.project-syndicate.org/commentary/a-new-deal-for-fragile-states-by-erik-solheim.
21 OECD (2002) listed 13 different conflict analysis frameworks.
22 Narrated by victim to Ofstad in March 1996.
23 Much of the advice on demobilisation and part of the discussion of reintegration are based on Faltas, 'Small arms – big problems' and Kingma, 'Demobilizing and reintegrating former combatants', in Reychler and Paffenholz (2001).
24 Rwanda is an example of the opposite, linking reconciliation to the establishment of an extensive special court system, called Gagaca. See Brounéus (2003).
25 Mari Alkatiri, East Timor's first prime minister, later called this a ticking time bomb (interview with Ofstad in June 2011).
26 USAID (2011) describes a reconciliation approach that is closely related to the model presented here.
27 Parts of the list are borrowed from Reychler, 'Conceptual framework', and Lund, 'A toolbox for responding to conflict', in Reychler and Pfaffenholz (2001).
28 UN staff Interviewed by Ofstad in June 2011.
29 www.google.com/search?sourceid=navclient&aq=hts&oq=&ie=UTF-8&rlz=1T4ADRA_enNO367NO368&q=Transitional+Appeals+Guidelines+%28UNDG%29.
30 Within the UN system, UNDAF plans and the UN Integrated Approach do go some way to facilitate coordination. The UN cluster approach, which in cases of emergency gathers groups of humanitarian organisations (UN and non-UN) working in nine different humanitarian sectors, including shelter, health, nutrition and logistics, is also a contribution. See http://business.un.org/en/documents/249.
31 Potentially effective systems for collection and sharing of information are the GIS based 'Sahana Eden', used by IFRC, and 'Tweak the Tweet,' a Twitter based tool for disaster response used inter alia in Haiti and Chile.
32 As earlier indicated (p. 101), one of the principles suggests that 'EU donors should confine their assistance in a partner country to two sectors in which they offer the best comparative advantage'.
33 OCHA's Strategic Framework for 2010–2013, http://unocha.org/annualreport/2011/strategic-plan.

34 World Bank staff interviewed by Ofstad in June 2006.
35 www.crisisgroup.org/en/regions/africa/horn-of-africa/112-beyond-victimhood-womens-peacebuilding-in-sudan-congo-and-uganda.aspx.
36 www.jovenescontralaviolencia.com/.

References

Anderson, M. (1999) *Do No Harm: How Aid Can Support Peace – or War*, London: Lynne Rienner.

Aronson, E., Wilson, T. D. and Akert, R. M. (1999) *Social Psychology*, New York: Addison-Wesley Longman.

Australian Aid, (2011) *Framework for Working in Fragile and Conflict-affected States*, http://aid.dfat.gov.au/Publications/Pages/1345_8687_9985_5238_2253.aspx.

Biersteker,T. J. (2007) *Prospects for the UN Peacebuilding Commission*, www.isn.ethz.ch/Digital-Library/Publications/Detail/?ots591=0c54e3b3–1e9c-be1e-2c24-a6a8c7060233&lng=en&id=47110.

Brehm, J. W. (1966) *A Theory of Psychological Reactance*, New York: Academic Press.

Brounéus, K. (2003) *Reconciliation – Theory and Practice for Development Cooperation*, www.pcr.uu.se/digitalAssets/18/18232_SIDA2982en_ReconWEB_brouneus.pdf.

Call, C. T. and Cousens, E. M. (2008) 'Ending wars and building peace: international responses to war-torn societies', *International Studies Perspectives* 9: 1–21, http://nw08.American.edu/~call/Publications/Ending%20Wars%20Building%20Peace.pdf.

Campbell, S. P. with Kayobera, L. and Nkurunziza, J. (2010) *Independent External Evaluation on Peacebuilding Fund Projects in Burundi*, http://graduateinstitute.ch/webdav/site/ccdp/shared/6305/Evaluation%20Burundi.pdf.

Caplan, R. (2005) *International Governance of War-torn Territories: Rule and Reconstruction*, Oxford: Oxford University Press.

CAVR (2005) *CHEGA! The CAVR Report*, www.cavr-timorleste.org/en/chegaReport.htm.

Curle, A. (1996) *Another Way: Positive Response to Contemporary Violence* Oxford: John Carpenter Publishing.

de Coning, C. (2009) *Implications of a Comprehensive or Integrated Approach for Training in United Nations and African Union's Peace Operations*, Security in Practice 6: Nupi Working Paper, www.nupi.no/Publikasjoner/Notater/2009/Implications-of-a-Comprehensive-or-Integrated-Approach-for-Training-in-United-Nations-and-African-Union-Peace-Operations.

de Coning, C. and de Carvalho, G. (2013) *Peacebuilding Handbook*, www.accord.org.za/our-work/peacebuilding/peacebuilding-handbook.

DFID (undated) *Building Peaceful States and Societies. A DFID Practice Paper*, www.gov.uk/government/publications/building-peaceful-states-and-societies-a-dfid-practice-paper.

European Union (2007) *Code of Conduct on Complementarity and the Division of Labour in Development Policy*, http://europa.eu/legislation_summaries/development/general_development_framework/r13003_en.htm.

Gheciu, A. and Welsh, J. (2009) 'The Imperative to Rebuild: Assessing the Normative Case for Post conflict Reconstruction', *Ethics & International Affairs* 23(2): 121–146.

G7+ (2011) *The New Deal*, www.g7plus.org/new-deal-document/.

Huyse, L. (2008) *Traditional Justice and Reconciliation after Violent Conflict. Learning from African Experiences*, Stockholm: International Institute for Democracy and

Electoral Assistance, www.idea.int/publications/traditional_justice/upload/Traditional_Justice_and_Reconciliation_after_Violent_Conflict.pdf.

International Crisis Group (2006) *Beyond Victimhood: Women's Peacebuilding in Sudan, Congo and Uganda*, Africa Report No. 112, Executive Summary and Recommendations.

Lederach, J. P. (1997) *Building Peace: Sustainable Reconciliation in Divided Societies*, Washington, DC: United States Institute of Peace.

Merson, M. H., Black, E. R. and Mills, J. A. (2006) *International Public Health*, 2nd edition, Sudbury: Jones and Bartlett.

NORAD (2004) *Peacebuilding: A Development Perspective: Strategic Framework*, www.norad.no/en/tools-and-publications/publications/publication?key=109522.

OECD (2002) *Guidance on Evaluating Conflict Prevention and Peacebuilding Activities*, www.oecd.org/secure/pdfDocument/0,2834,en_21571361_34047972_39774574_1_1_1_1,00.pdf.

OECD/DAC (2012) *Evaluating Peacebuilding Activities in Settings of Conflict and Fragility, Guidelines and Reference Series*, www.oecd.org/dac/evaluation/evaluatingconflictpreventionandpeacebuilding.htm.

Ofstad, O. (2012) *Reconciliation and Conflict Resolution in East Timor:, Lessons for Future Operations*, www.elac.ox.ac.uk/downloads/Reconciliation%20and%20conflict%20resoloution %20 in%20East%20Timor%20Apr%202012.pdf.

Ramsbotham, O., Wodhouse, T., and Miall, H. (2011) *Contemporary Conflct Resolution*, Polity Press Maiden

Reeve, R. (2012) *Peace and Conflict Assessment of South Sudan*, http://concordis-international.org/wp-content/uploads/2012/11/International-Alert-Peace-and-Conflict-Assessment-South-Sudan-2012.pdf.

Reychler, L. and Paffenholz, T. (2001) *Peace-building. A Field Guide*, London: Lynne Rienner.

Scambary, J. (2009) 'Anatomy of a conflict: the 2006–2007 communal violence in East Timor', *Conflict, Security and Development* 9(2): 265–288.

SIDA (2006) *Manual for Conflict Analysis*, www.conflictsensitivity.org/sites/default/files/Manual_for_Conflict_Analysis.pdf.

SIDA (2012) *HRBA and Peace Building. A Human Rights Based Approach to Peace Building*, www.peacebuildinginitiative.org/index.cfm?pageId=1848.

Smith, D. (2004) *Towards a Strategic Framework for Peacebuilding: Getting Their Act Together. Overview Report of the Joint Utstein Study of Peacebuilding*, Oslo: PRIO – International Peace Research Institute for NORAD, www.norad.no/en/tools-and-publications/publications/publication?key=165470.

Smith, M. G. with Dee, M. (2003) *Peacekeeping in East Timor. The Path to Independence*, London: Lynne Rienner.

Solli, A., de Carvalho, B., de Coning, C. and Pedersen, M. F. (2011) 'Training in vain? Bottlenecks in deploying civilians for UN peacekeeping', *International Peacekeeping* 18(4), www.tandfonline.com/doi/abs/10.1080/13533312.2011.588389journal/Code=finp20.

Trinidade, J. and Castro, B. (2007) *Technical Assistance to the National Dialogue Process in Timor-Leste: Rethinking Timorese Identity as a Peacebuilding Strategy: The Lorosa'e–Loromonu Conflict from a Traditional Perspective*, www.indopubs.com/Trindade_Castro_Rethinking_Timorese_Identity.pdf.

UNDG/ECHA (2004) *Interagency Framework for Conflict Analysis in Transition Situations*, www.google.co.uk/#q=As+part+of+the+follow-up+from+the+Joint+UNDG-

ECHA+Working+Group+on+Transition%2C+the+Implementation+Plan+calls+for+the+creation+of+a+framework+for+a+common+contextual+analysis+for+the+causes+of+conflict%2C+.

UN Peacebuilding Fund (2007) *Priority Plan for Peacebuilding in Burundi, Strategic Note*, February 2007, PBSO-6 March 2007, www.peacebuilderscenter.jp/parts/20101213–17/20101214Material_Takeuchi.pdf.

UN Peacebuilding Commission (2007) *Strategic Framework for Peacebuilding in Burundi*, PBC/1/BDI/4 (21 June 2007).

UN Peacebuilding Fund (2011) *Draft Liberia Peacebuilding Programme*, www.unpbf.org/countries/liberia.

USAID (2011) *People-to-People Peacebuilding: A Programme Guide*, www.usaid.gov/sites/default/files/documents/1866/CMMP2PGuidelines2010–01–19.pdf.

Vaux, T., Goodhand, J. and Walker, R. (2002) *Conducting Conflict Assessments: Guidance Notes*, London: DFID, www.conflictsensitivity.org/publications/conducting-conflict-assessments-guidance-notes.

Verghese, A. and Kelly J. (2012) *OSCE Talks*: *Preparing for Peace. Communications in Conflict Resolution*, www.osce.org/secretariat/98116?download=true.

Wilson, C. (2005) Overlooking Violent Conflict. Peace and Development (DPA) in Indonesia, Jakarta: UNDP.

Woodhouse, T. and Duffey, T. (2009) *Peacekeeping and International Conflict Resolution*, www.peaceopstraining.org/.

World Bank (2011) *The World Development Report*, http://web.worldbank.org/WBSITE/EXTERNAL/EXTDEC/EXTRESEARCH/EXTWDRS/0,,contentMDK:23252415~pagePK:478093~piPK:477627~theSitePK:477624,00.html.

Zaum, D. (2007) *The Sovereignty Paradox: The Sovereignty Paradox: The Norms and Politics of International Statebuilding*, Oxford: Oxford University Press.

7 When you or your agency becomes party to a conflict

We all become party to conflicts. We have differences with friends, family, colleagues, neighbours, tax authorities, etc. The possibilities are limitless. Let us take a look at a situation where you are involved in a conflict, first personally, then as a representative of your agency.

The contents of Chapter 4, 'Mediation', also have relevance for our own conflicts. So has everything on communication and traditional approaches presented in Chapter 5. As we shall see below, the use of influence psychology may, however, subject to the situation, be ethically problematic.

Personal conflicts

Handling a conflict is more difficult when you are a party to it. This is because we are easily affected by our emotions, and this influences our ability to think rationally. We all know the saying 'It is easier to raise the kids of others', and most of us have experienced how difficult it can be to act sensibly when in conflict with someone we love.

A major challenge in personal conflicts is therefore to assess the situation objectively. To make it simple, let us assume that you have only one counterpart.

Calm down and wait

Avoid raising conflicts spontaneously. Psychological research indicates that in general communication between the parties only helps so long as the intensity of the conflict is relatively low (Pruitt and Rubin, 1986). If you embark on communication while you are angry or upset, you can be almost sure that things will go wrong and the possibilities of a positive outcome will be ruined. In other words, wait till you are at ease. A few days' break may be good.

In the meantime, do some introspection. Maybe you have overreacted? Is this issue as important as you felt initially? Take a look at the contents of the conflict. Could there be some misunderstanding? Have you understood what your opponent means? Do you know the interests underlying her position? Sometimes conflicts die by themselves if we take time to ask these questions.

Raising the problem

Let us assume you have taken time to calm down. You have thought through the subject and your own attitude, and tried your best to understand your opponent. It is time to talk.

Raise what you perceive as a conflict, but be careful not to call it that. Many perceive 'conflict' as a heavy term. Try to use harmless wording when describing the issue. Avoid accusing your counterpart of anything. A good start may be simply to say there is something you feel a need to improve or look at together.

If you and your opponent agree on the need for improvement or discussion, try to assume joint responsibility for the process. This will enhance the chances of success. Together, you may also try to establish the likely outcome if you don't achieve a positive change; but, as emphasised earlier, a positive focus is essential.

Is dialogue or mediation most relevant?

Do you know anyone who would fit the role of mediator? It is often wise to seek assistance, but we may feel that mediation in a private conflict is a little too formal and complicated, perhaps also embarrassing. Here, we shall assume that you agree to discuss the conflict alone.

Try to agree on the purpose of your discussion. This may be to find practical solutions or changes, but also simply to understand each other. (If each party commits to try to understand the other, you have a good basis for positive change.) Set aside plenty of time and find a quiet place.

Should you agree on a strategy? In a personal conflict it may often seem too formal to define a strategy for the process. If not, you might suggest a slightly simplified approach, like:

1 presentation and clarification
2 identifying interests
3 finding ways of meeting interests
4 seeking solutions
5 agreement and follow-up.

'Traffic rules' are also important in personal conflicts. If you manage to agree on joint responsibility, you should also commit yourselves to:

- discriminating between case and person
- avoiding accusations
- listening to the other without interruption
- trying to understand each other
- helping each other with the process towards a positive outcome.

Presentation and clarification

Most of what was said about the mediation process also applies here. The difference is that you have to run it together. You might not have a flip-chart but use a notepad to take down what you find in terms of agreement and disagreement, positions, interests, etc.

Everything we have said about good communication and empathy (p. 71) should be observed. Invite your counterpart to explain his position first. That shows a serious interest from your side and has a reassuring effect. It may also add to your own feeling of responsibility. Ask whatever questions are required to make sure you fully understand his position and views. If you are good at paraphrasing (p. 71) you may use this tool if the atmosphere allows it. This may diffuse tension and clarify the subject. Next, present your own position. Be receptive to questions and remember to highlight any agreement you can identify.

Shortcuts to resolution

At times we may find it difficult to discuss personal conflicts constructively, perhaps because the issue is too sensitive or we need a solution fast. If you can think of a solution you believe is acceptable to your counterpart, you may be better off skipping the identification of interests (and also emotions) and simply going straight to your proposal: 'Is it OK if we do it like this in future?' This approach has the advantage that no blame is expressed whatsoever.

Identifying interests

Unless you have chosen the shortcut approach and succeeded, you should invite your counterpart to explain his interests. As earlier observed, these may be interests that caused the conflict but are not necessarily. Today the prime interest may be, for instance, reconciliation.

We may not always be clear on what we really need. Help your counterpart with the identification process as far as you can. If the atmosphere is good you might perhaps draw up a list of basic human needs together?

Advice on communication

Be aware that in personal conflicts interests and needs may easily come across as offensive or hurtful. If you tell your roommate that you need more silence, he might easily feel labelled as noisy, even if migraine is your problem. And if your loved one says she needs more freedom, you may believe she sees you as possessive or boring, even if her need is self-realisation. So be prepared to muster some strength when hearing your counterpart out on interests.

Before expressing your own interests, take some time to find formulations that do not hurt or blame. Even if you think your counterpart is to blame, you must avoid assigning guilt and responsibility. Only then can you expect an open and positive response.

Exchanging feelings in a balanced way can sometimes contribute to an atmosphere of compassion. Whether you have agreed on such exchanges or not, emotions often surface. But beware: few people know the art of expressing emotions in a personal conflict without hurting or offending the other party. And personal conflicts sometimes contain more emotions than we are aware of. So if exchanging feelings, be prepared for the worst, and commit yourself to staying cool.

Expressing our own emotions is a challenge even if you have been trained in communication or conflict management. Particularly if we feel hurt or provoked, it may be difficult to say so without making your counterpart feel blamed. It is therefore imperative that you take time to find formulations that won't hurt or provoke. Avoid formulations that point at the other party.

The choice of verbs is essential. If you say, 'I felt let down after our conversation', your counterpart will most likely feel accused of letting you down. You are more likely to get a positive response if you say: 'I felt bad after our conversation. How did you feel?'

Our feelings are, in general, linked to our needs. If you are able to do it in a balanced way, refer to your needs instead of your counterpart's statements or behaviour.

Let us say an old friend has given you a scolding. You are upset and concerned about your friendship. If you tell him that his scolding made you upset, he may not be very receptive. Perhaps he thinks he did not scold you at all or that you deserved every bit of it. But you might also say: 'I felt uneasy after our discussion because I need to know we are still friends'. With this approach you avoid blame and your friend is more likely to respond with empathy.

Our context does not allow a profound discussion of this subject. But summing up, the main advice must be: take time, assess your wording and avoid anything that could be perceived as blame or accusation.[1]

Meeting interests/seeking solutions

If you have been able to identify both parties' interests, you should work together to find ways of meeting them. The more empathy and cooperation, the better the chances of success. For advice on the process, see p. 48.

Based on your findings as to possible ways of meeting both parties' interests, you may now explore possible solutions. Again, you should cooperate closely. As for the process of solution, take a look at the suggestions in Chapter 4. Even if a dialogue may be simpler than a mediated process, most of the advice on pp. 49–54 is relevant. Unless your counterpart is an experienced conflict manager, you may have to pose the relevant questions. Remember to apply a neutral form like:

- Should we try the miracle question?
- Do you think it is a good idea to involve subjects from outside the conflict?
- Should we try to develop combinations of needs coverage?

Remember that a joint brainstorming session (p. 51) can be very productive. If your counterpart is negative about this approach, you might suggest that you take a break and do it separately, or that you both do it before the next meeting.

How cooperative should you be?

Both Fisher and Ury (1991) and Pruitt and Rubin (1986) recommend that after analysing your own needs, you should commit yourself to them. In other words, you should have a good reserve of persistence or stubbornness. Fisher and Ury (1991: 54) even suggest that 'This is the place in a negotiation to spend your aggressive energies.'

The advantage of this attitude is that you really invest in the process, and that you don't easily risk entering into an agreement you may regret later. However, if the parties have come to understand each other's interests and agree on joint efforts to meet them, there will be less need for stubbornness. And aggression is in general likely to jeopardise the tone of cooperation.

The suggestion of persistence otherwise seems to disregard the possibility that your opponent's needs are more legitimate than your own, and you should be aware of a possible imbalance. If for instance you need aspirin after a heavy party, and your roommate needs it for the diffusion of blood after a heart attack, you will hopefully not be very stubborn.

Under all circumstances, be flexible about how your needs are fulfilled. Moreover, if you and your counterpart are seeking a position-based solution, this may demand flexibility in the sense of renunciation. The main point here is the balance between the parties.

If you find yourselves deadlocked, try to withdraw mentally from the problem. Suggest to your counterpart that you take a break and that you both pretend the conflict is new to you. Try to identify entirely new angles to see what possibilities might open up.

What kind of solution?

Position-based solutions where both parties' positions are fully met are rare, and compromises, where only certain parts of the parties' claims are fulfilled, often constitute bad solutions.

Interest-based solutions are, as previously observed, normally the best outcome you can hope for.

Objective criteria may offer an option if neither position-based nor interest-based solutions seem satisfactory. If so, the best option may be to agree on objective criteria, such as: 'What does the law or the agreement say?'

An agreed form of resolution such as throwing a dice may be practical if there are only two alternatives, and if both parties concur on such a method. For example, 'Who is to drive the best car?' or 'Who is to do the field trip on Saturday?'

When searching for a solution or understanding, make sure you establish clearly what you agree on. Writing something down contributes to clarity and a feeling of mutual commitment. If appropriate, agree on a time to meet again to follow up together, to ensure that you implement what you agreed.

Use of influence psychology

The mechanisms depicted in Chapter 5 may in principle be used. The advice given on the use of influence psychology is meant for particular challenges, however, such as addressing abuse or violence. If you are the victim in such a conflict, you may of course try to use those techniques. But in less dramatic conflicts between two equal parties such techniques may lose much of their ethical justification and could, depending on the situation, become contentious. This is why we have chosen here to focus on another approach, where the parties deal with the conflict as a joint challenge.

Two aspects of influence psychology might, however, be observed:

- If the parties dislike each other strongly, you may try to improve the situation through cognitive dissonance (pp. 66–68). Remember that if you do something positive for a person you dislike, you will probably like him a little better afterwards. And if you can motivate a person to do something positive for you, then she may begin to like you better. Such acts may subdue the feeling of conflict and make it easier to address it together.
- It is worth remembering the significance of roles (p. 61). If both parties assume the role of conflict manager with responsibility for the result, you may be on your way to a positive outcome.

Your agency as party to a conflict

International agencies sometimes become party to conflicts. Typical situations are the distribution of provisions to civilians, protection of refugees, repatriation, etc., all of which may imply or lead to conflicts with groups or individuals in the local society. The conflict may affect the entire organisation or involve only your local unit. Negotiations may be required to solve the conflict or avoid escalation. Please observe that most of the advice given in Chapter 4 is also relevant here.

Your role as a negotiator is different from that of a mediator

In mediation, you are supposed to be impartial, and the objective is to help the parties reach a peaceful settlement or positive development. When negotiating for an international organisation, you represent a party to the conflict and are obliged to actively seek a result or development that complies with your organisation's mission and interests. To this end, you need to work in conjunction with your line of command.

What about using influence psychology in this kind of conflict?

The concerns about using influencing techniques when handling personal conflicts also apply here. But if your agency is party to the conflict, it is perhaps more likely that you will find the use of such techniques ethically acceptable.

Preparing for negotiations

What we observed about preparation for mediation (p. 40) also applies here. You must understand the conflict fully but you are in particular responsible for knowing the positions and attitudes of your agency. Unless the conflict is new, there might be documents on the case, perhaps also instructions. Make sure you know beforehand what you are authorised to negotiate on, and what has to be endorsed by your superiors.

Preparing a delegation

If this is your responsibility, you have to clarify the roles. Who is to attend? Who is to do the representation?

Do you have to bring experts, such as technical or legal ones? Remember to bring good interpreters. Make sure all are well prepared for their tasks. If you have more than one counterpart, you should normally try to meet them one at a time. Meetings with more than one person may be hard to handle, and should only happen if the atmosphere between the parties allows it.

Remember also that it is a strategic advantage to meet on home ground. This may also allow you to break the ice by gestures such as an introduction to your colleagues and lunch during the main break.

Security requirements

Negotiation scenes may vary a lot, and must be subjected to concrete assessment. You may wish to confer with peacekeeping forces, UN police or local police about the security situation and possible support. The security details must in any case be handled well, so that all participants feel secure during the meeting as well as while travelling to and from the venue. Three main questions should be thoroughly considered:

- What is the security situation in the area? Is there any reason to fear attacks?
- Are special measures required as to guards and control of access to the meeting place?
- How are the participants to be evacuated if necessary?

Introductory phase

If the meeting takes place on your 'home ground', start by welcoming your counterpart and express appreciation that you are meeting for discussions.

Introduce your delegation. Remember to be polite and use people's titles. Some small talk and humour are also recommended here.

Is anyone going to chair the negotiations?

In principle, one can imagine using a neutral mediator or chairperson, but the role and authority of your organisation may render this unnatural. Here we are going to look at negotiations without a mediator or chairperson.

FRAMES AND STRATEGY

Discuss the goal of the negotiations and agree on a joint statement if possible. Clarify together whether you need a strategy for the process. In line with what we have earlier suggested, your proposal might be:

1 presentation of positions
2 clarifying the problem
3 identifying interests
4 ways of meeting interests
5 seeking solutions
6 drawing up an agreement
7 following up.

If the issue is complex, you may have to agree on a series of meetings and the content of these. In any case, agree on a purpose and a schedule for the first meeting, including breaks, summing up and signing minutes.

'Traffic rules' must be agreed. Agree on limited speaking time, a ban on offensive languages and interruptions. Both parties should explicitly endorse these rules.

Minutes should be taken. Agree on who should take minutes, what to include and what language to use. Agree that you both sign the minutes at the end of the meeting.

Presentations

Invite your counterpart to present his case first. Note the main points and possible factual errors, but do not interrupt, even if accused or insulted.

When doing your own presentation you should start by summing up your counterpart's position to avoid possible misunderstandings. Use the paraphrasing technique (p. 71) if you can master it. You should correct factual errors and you may wish to reject insults, but do so in a balanced manner.

Underscore issues where you both agree, and try to clarify the disagreement as well as you can.

Be prepared to help in clarifying the problem. If your counterpart accepts it, you may take a lead in this. Start by stating points of agreement. Note these on a flip-chart that you put up on the wall.

Identify points of disagreement together, and agree to address them point by point. Revisit the advice given in Chapter 4.

Expressing emotions

Negotiations on behalf on your organisation will be more formal than discussions on personal conflicts. You will recall that exchange of emotions may have a tension-diffusing effect, but only if the parties avoid becoming provoked. For your part, you should show constraint in expressing negative feelings such as anger or frustration, since any expression may be perceived as representative of your organisation. As for positive feelings such as joy or satisfaction, there are no such concerns. Remember also the benefits of showing empathy.

Shortcuts to a resolution

Sometimes solutions may appear in the early phases of negotiations. All of a sudden it strikes the parties that 'this is the way we can do it!' If you see such a possibility early on, you may agree with your counterpart to pursue it there and then, and abandon the more thorough interest-based approach.

Identifying interests

Unless you have identified a possible shortcut, you now invite your counterpart to present his interests. Depending on his experience with conflict handling, you should be prepared to help him actively both to identify interests and to discriminate between interests and positions. Be open to any interest he presents.

You will recall from mediation that the underlying interests should be listed under the positions, using one flip-chart page per position.

When addressing the interests of your organisation you face a different aspect. Underneath these interests lie a strategy, perhaps a mandate and possibly instructions. In a way you could say these are your agency's 'basic needs'.

Let us assume that you have been assigned to supply a refugee camp with food and medicines. You may wish to use trucks on a private road built by villagers in the neighbourhood. They do not want your organisation to use it, since they use the road for goods transport themselves and fear heavy vehicles might destroy it. Their interests may pertain to trade and transport of provisions for their village, while their basic needs are food, clothing, etc. Can their interests be met while you fulfil your mandate?

If your position is not based on strategy, mandate or instructions, your interest may simply be to meet the interests of your beneficiaries.

Ways of meeting interests

For your counterpart in the road conflict, the question is: how can our interests be met? You should ask the villagers to identify all possible approaches that may meet their interests. Help them with this if required, and try to agree that the identification process does not commit them to any particular approach.

For you, the question is: in what ways can my mission be fulfilled? Alternatively, how can I meet the needs of our beneficiaries?

This could happen in different ways. The obvious idea that you repair the road when the operations are over may not be enough if the villagers' use of the road is impeded for a longer period. You might in principle consider an offer from the villagers to rent smaller vehicles to you or even camels or oxcarts. Perhaps you might be able to use boats or drop provisions from a plane? Imagination might reveal a variety of possibilities.

Seeking solutions

You will recall that solutions may be defined in various ways. They may be based on one single way of meeting interests or a combination of ways, perhaps with a range of values and concessions added, or one may opt for a simple solution technique, such as applying objective criteria.

The villagers are free to 'juggle' with different ways of meeting their own interests, and they may, in principle, go for any conceivable measure or approach that fulfils their interests.

You don't have the same freedom. Observing your mission or assignment, you have to provide the refugees with provisions. For instance, you cannot accept as a solution that they are to fish in the river and grow vegetables, or make their own herbal medicines.

Can expanding the cake help?

Is there anything you could possibly offer your counterpart, within or outside the scope of conflict, which might be of interest to them? Maybe they are in need of provisions that you have in excess in your warehouse? Perhaps your mechanics could help them repair their defunct tractor? But remember the warning against making commitments you cannot live up to. Also remember, when acting as a party, to make sure all your offers are authorised or within your mandate.

The solution process is essentially as outlined on pp. 49–54.

However, you and your counterpart will have to explore solutions jointly. Brainstorming may also be effective here. You may, in that case, have to suggest that you address together the questions listed on p. 50.

If you find that a joint brainstorming session clashes with the authority and respect you need, you might try to do it alone or with your negotiation team.

Forms of resolution

As in other conflicts, one may imagine the following forms of solution.

Position-based solutions, where both parties positions are met, are rarely achievable in this context. In the conflict over the road, you cannot possibly meet both parties' positions in full. Compromise is conceivable, for example limiting your access to the road.

Interest-based solutions are again normally the best outcome. The road conflict will probably offer several possible interest-based solutions.

Using objective criteria could also be an option. In the road conflict you may, for example, agree to explore whether the villagers own the road or have exclusive rights to it according to the law or public registries.

Agreeing on resolution techniques like arbitration or tossing a coin is in principle an option but could be tricky in this context. Such approaches are only acceptable if you are sure the result will not clash with your mandate or assignment.

Minutes and agreement

As indicated above, the choice of language and the responsibility for taking minutes should be agreed with your counterpart at the beginning of the meeting. Sometimes the situation or the time aspect may prevent you from taking minutes during the meeting. If so, you should take time afterwards to work on the wording and ensure clarity and accuracy. You may then have the minutes taken to your counterpart for signature or take them with you to the next meeting.

Any agreement must be as clear as possible. Who is to do what and when? What follow-up should be agreed?

The language should be one that is used internationally, preferably the working language of your organisation. For your counterpart, a version in the local language may be required, but the terms should state that the international version prevails.

Remember that most agreements need active follow-up, some over a longer period of time. Make your own time schedule and note down all planned activities. Otherwise observe the advice on follow-up provided in Chapter 4.

Personal security and danger signals

International organisations are not popular with everyone. Some may not see their interests served by peace and reconciliation; others may dislike the presence of international actors. This might be about reluctance to accept external interference in general, disapproval of a UN mandate, etc.

There may also be a repugnance towards your organisation as such or its local presence. This could be about the work you do. For example, human rights organisations are not popular with everyone. You could also be seen as representatives of cultural or economic imperialism, or as agents of hostile countries.

In recent times there have been increasing attacks on international workers, including murders and kidnapping for ransom and/or political purposes. You, personally, could also get involved in dangerous conflict situations with local groups or people.

Let us imagine that hostility against your organisation is mounting in the local society. This may stem from insurgents, political actors, religious groups or different civilian interest groups or persons. It may materialise in different ways, such as threats, agitation, etc. We shall assume that you get to know what is happening before it turns violent.

Conflicts between your agency and local groups

Identifying your adversary is sometimes a challenge

In December 1996, six Red Cross delegates were killed in a night-time attack on a hospital in Chechnya. It was never established for certain who was behind it.

From time to time organisations face dangerous emotional developments in local society without knowing their origin. Sometimes groups oppose the international presence without making their views known. If you notice antagonism developing, your first challenge may be identification. Is this about a known group? Who are the key persons or opinion leaders? Where are they based? Can any of your contacts in the local society, possibly UN police or representatives of other international organisations, help you identify them?

Let us assume you find out who 'the enemy' is. Mediation will normally be a non-issue. So what to do? If the situation represents a credible threat to your or others' lives, evacuation might be required. Not all antagonism is life-threatening, however, and before thinking of pulling out, your organisation would normally wish to determine whether the situation can be handled in the field.

USE OF GO-BETWEENS

Could you have others intervene? Can international partners help? Provided you have done a good job in establishing local contacts, then perhaps they may exert influence? If not, you will have to handle the problem yourself in conjunction with your superiors. But even if others do intervene, it may be wise to take an initiative of your own. If security allows it, this means you should consider the possibility of establishing contact with your opponent.

MEET 'THE ENEMY'

The meeting must of course be safe, and be organised in conjunction with your superiors. Normally a hostile person will not accept an invitation to your office. That means the venue must be at your counterpart's or someone else's place.

If it is safe to do so, visit your opponent, and remember to describe it as a courtesy call. If we assume you are meeting your 'enemy' for the first time, what do you say to him? The advice given about initial courtesy calls (p. 34) is relevant here. A soft approach is advisable. Introduce your organisation and its mission. Explain what you are doing and that you wish to cooperate with important groups and persons.

The criticism may be expressed spontaneously. If not, ask for his view on the international presence or the work of your organisation. Receive the criticism in a positive way. You might wish to thank him for his frank opinion. Make it clear that you want a dialogue. Use the opportunity to build confidence as far as possible. Follow the advice on meetings with negative persons (p. 36). The purpose is that at the end of the meeting you leave the kind of positive impression outlined under 'Courtesy calls' (pp. 35–36). You will have made it clear that your organisation or unit is in the country strictly to support its people. You have shown your face and demonstrated that you work for peace. You have appeared as a good listener with an interest in your counterpart's view and a general understanding of other people. If possible, raise the issue of keeping in contact in the future.

Even if your counterpart disapproves of both your agency and its work, you will have achieved a minimum level of respect, both as a person and as a representative of your agency. All in all, you will have made it more difficult for him to obstruct your work, let alone launch a physical attack against your organisation.

Conflicts between you and local persons/groups

A repatriation officer with the UNHCR in Croatia/Bosnia received serious threats after having managed the closure of a refugee camp, where the inhabitants, despite their protests, were dispersed to other camps. For some time she had to avoid certain parts of her mandate area. After a while her colleagues established contact with a political leader of the refugees, who, after some discussions, agreed to spread the word that the officer must be left in peace. She was then able to resume her work in the actual area.

Some of your activities may lead to negative reactions in the local society. You may have handed out emergency rations without having enough for everyone, or selected one of two villages in conflict for a development project. Such acts may be enough to provoke aggression towards you as a person and in the worst case the situation may become dangerous. If you are a party to the conflict it becomes even more important that you do not handle it alone. In case of threats towards you, your superiors/your organisation's security officer must be briefed immediately.

The normal approach in this case will be to assess whether the situation can be handled in the field, but your superior and security staff should support you to the necessary extent, and eventually make a decision on how to ensure your security. Unfortunately, sometimes leaders leave it to the exposed person in the field to make a decision on evacuation, as they feel she is better positioned to assess the risk. If so, do not try to be a hero. A number of delegates have been harmed because they did not heed warnings. Try to step outside yourself and ask, 'If I were the one to provide honest advice in this situation, what would it be?'

A comprehensive discussion of security aspects related to conflict exceeds the scope of this book. While there is limited literature focusing specifically on this topic, a number of related challenges are discussed in Roberts (1999).

Note

1 For further guidance on communication on needs and emotions, see Rosenberg (1999).

References

Fisher, R. and Ury, W. (1991) *Getting to Yes*, New York: Penguin Books.

Pruitt, D. G. and Rubin, J. Z. (1986) *Social Conflict, Escalation, Stalemate and Settlement*, New York: Random House.

Roberts, D. L. (1999) *Staying Alive. Safety and Security Guidelines for Humanitarian Volunteers in Conflict Areas*, Geneva: ICRC.

Rosenberg, M. B. (1999) *Nonviolent Communication. A Language of Compassion*, Del Mar, CA: Puddle Dancer Press.

Conclusions

The prime intention of this book is to serve as a guide for preparations for missions, settlement in the field and handling of any conflict-related challenges you may face, including the multifaceted challenges of peacebuilding.

However, conflict management is also a life skill, and the book has introduced you to concepts that may be as useful in personal contexts as they are in professional situations.

Admittedly, some topics might be a bit complex and human memory does not store the contents of books for ever. But hopefully you will use the index and revisit relevant topics when needed. While all the book's contents are there for a purpose, certain elements justify some extra attention. Let us revisit the chapters.

Chapter 1: What you should know about conflicts

It is important to understand the concepts of position, interests and basic human needs. Such factors can be found in any kind of conflict, as a basis for dialogue, negotiations or mediation. But remember that antagonism may exist without visible difference in interest. In such cases reconciliation and sometimes psychological influence are the most adequate means.

Some of the book's conflict terminology differs from that of other writers. But remember that no one owns definitions. You are free to use your own. The main point is to give the terms enough conscious thought to be clear in your mind about their meaning as you relate to them later.

Communication is a key element of the book. Whatever conflict issues you face, constructive, peaceful interaction requires good communication skills. So please review the sections addressing communication carefully, particularly pp. 71–73.

Chapter 2: Preparing for missions

Your responsibilities and allegiances could be numerous, and the range of relevant documents/international norms may seem daunting to first-timers. However, a proper discussion with your line of command will normally go a long way to clear the picture.

Remember that the 'Do no harm' concepts are important reading for anyone involved in humanitarian activities in conflict zones.

The need for knowledge of local history, culture/traditions and religion and ethnicity is generally important when working abroad, and more so when one is involved in conflict management.

Use all the time available to learn before starting your mission. Once you are out in the field, things might be too hectic.

'Principles under pressure' is a reminder that conflict management is a difficult business, and success is never guaranteed. Sometimes finding a good approach to the conflict itself is the easiest part. Power/legitimacy issues, corruption, mistrust and other factors sometimes frustrate the best efforts.

Chapter 3: Establishing yourself in the field

You will probably need to gain more local knowledge than you were able to pick up before your departure. If possible, make space for this early on. You may engage one or more local resource persons for a seminar, but beware of their relationship with the parties to the conflicts.

We should all seek optimal results for our efforts, and defining a personal strategy is one way to go about it. Ask yourself what you can achieve, given your position, resources and known challenges, and make it your personal commitment.

The question 'What kind of peace?' is about the ethics of peacebuilding. We should only support the reforms that our local partners understand, need and want. This can easily become a challenge in a democracy perspective.

Establishing local contacts is normally essential for successful field work. If you have problems in this regard, revisit the advice given on p. 36.

Chapter 4: Mediation

A full-scale structured mediation can be quite complicated. If you have been engaged as mediator, make sure you read this chapter carefully before the process starts and keep the basics clear in your mind. You might keep this book close at hand and use breaks for a quick refresher. Take control from the start and agree with the parties on your purpose, plans and traffic rules.

If you miss out on these aspects, success is unlikely and deterioration of the conflict may be the outcome.

At the same time, stay flexible as you progress, and be open to shortcuts to solutions.

Even in less formal, simpler mediation or negotiation contexts, the advice given in this chapter will be useful.

Chapter 5: Influence: psychology vs traditional approaches

The advice given in this chapter is essential in contexts where you have to influence parties to a conflict. A typical challenge is to stop a stronger party from abusing a weaker one. Particularly effective tools are role expectations and cognitive dissonance. To make sure you learn the main techniques, you may try them out in 'peacetime', in interaction with friends, family or colleagues.

If you are looking at ways to influence events over time, make your own little strategy, defining how you will use the different tools of this chapter.

Use the above mentioned section, 'on good communication'. Remember that your counterpart has basic human needs that should be observed, including respect and understanding. But also remember that you must command respect yourself.

Unfortunately, social psychology has no strong standing in international politics, and the traditional approaches of influence discussed in this chapter are generally not very appropriate.

Chapter 6: Peacebuilding

You will by now have a good understanding of what peacebuilding is about. Hopefully you will also use the book as support when relating to the different phases and tasks. But be warned that some aspects are likely to pose challenges regardless of your knowledge.

Analysis

We have observed that national peacebuilding efforts require comprehensive, multidisciplinary needs analysis and conflict analysis, and neither is common.

Some agencies conduct their own analysis, which may serve their needs but cannot replace the analysis governments require for the overall planning of peacebuilding.

To define needs and/or conflicts in the context you work in, you may conduct your own analysis, possibly in conjunction with colleagues, in line with the guidance offered on p. 113.

Plans

The analyses should feed into comprehensive peacebuilding plans, defining how needs should be met and conflicts and antagonism addressed. These might be part of development plans, but all peacebuilding needs must be included. Such plans are not common. Peacebuilding elements such as national reconciliation are often mentioned in development plans or poverty reduction strategies, but with limited action defined.

If you are providing high-level support to government planning, you might try to inspire your counterparts to take peacebuilding planning seriously.

Through the 2006 architecture and other developments, the UN has boosted its capacity to support national peacebuilding planning, but its contributions need assessment.

On a programme and project level we should always consult government representatives or peacebuilding leadership about our intentions and ideas before we complete our own planning. However, lack of overall strategic and programmatic parameters is often a handicap. The practical consequences of inadequate analysis and poor planning can be numerous.

Conflict resolution and reconciliation

These elements often suffer. East Timor is one such example. Truth and reconciliation commissions may be mentioned in plans or frameworks, but implementation might never happen.

During high-level cooperation with the government, we may raise the importance of large-scale reconciliation. However, the UN's commitment to linking justice and reconciliation is often an obstacle, given state leaders' desire to protect their followers.

At programme level your agency is free to suggest any contribution to reconciliation, and this chapter presents a range of possibilities, including a model for cooperation between adversaries.

Coordination

The essence of coordination as presented here is 'to adapt, integrate and facilitate activities towards the most effective needs coverage possible'. However, we cannot coordinate for needs we do not know of, and the lack of needs mapping/analysis is a general handicap. The lack of overall peacebuilding plans is another problem, as strategic and programmatic direction may be missing.

Consequently, coordination may be about making the best of whatever knowledge is accessible, providing mutual support and using whatever possibilities for cooperation we can find. The list of questions/topics on pp. 140–141 will hopefully be useful.

Given the ongoing electronic information revolution, our efforts at coordination will hopefully become more technically advanced in the near future, but at present there are striking unutilised possibilities.

Chapter 7: When you or your agency becomes party to a conflict

You will have observed that conflicts in different contexts and at different levels have basic similarities, in that they are always about human beings, their motives, interests and emotions. All conflict management is based on these basic facts and therefore includes similarities.

One special factor in agency contexts is that your mandate may be the 'interests' you have to pursue. Personal conflicts are often very emotional, and the biblical saying 'Don't let the sun go down on your anger' addresses this fact. The suggestion here is the opposite. While you are angry, you are ill-equipped to resolve conflicts, so spend at least one sunset calming down and thinking through the issue before you raise the problem.

The mechanisms of psychological influence discussed in Chapter 5 are in principle applicable in any conflict, but the ethical justification for using them may be a problem, particularly in personal conflicts.

However, it is hardly contentious to use them to reduce tension and improve relationships. (Remember Benjamin Franklin, p. 67).

Discussions of security related to conflict are limited to certain interpersonal aspects that you may have to address, for instance by 'meeting your enemy' if it is not dangerous.

Future perspectives

Some of the topics discussed in this book are under constant development. Peacebuilding stands out in that UN institutions and practices have changed in recent years. Other major actors such as the EU and the African Union have assumed more responsibility, and a number of international agencies have taken a more analytical approach to their own work.

Specific conflict management topics such as mediation and negotiations are also being subjected to research and discussions, although ground-breaking developments may be rare.

Clearly, the world needs to progress in all the fields we have discussed. To this end, anyone understanding essential concepts and challenges should contribute, and hopefully you will be part of the discussions.

Index

Page numbers in *italics* denote tables.

For Product Safety Concerns and Information please contact our EU representative GPSR@taylorandfrancis.com Taylor & Francis Verlag GmbH, Kaufingerstraße 24, 80331 München, Germany